SPECIAL NEEDS
in the early years

The essential A–Z guide
to special needs

INFORMATION ON TERMS AND CONDITIONS • HOW YOU CAN HELP • WHERE TO GO TO FIND OUT MORE

The King is very happy.

DR HANNAH MORTIMER

Author
Dr Hannah Mortimer

Editor
Victoria Lee

Assistant Editor
Aileen Lalor

Series Designers
Sarah Rock/Anna Oliwa

Designer
Andrea Lewis

Illustrations
Shelagh McNicholas

Cover artwork
Claire Henley

Acknowledgements
Extracts from the Education Act 1996 (Section 312) © Crown Copyright

Every effort has been made to trace copyright holders and the publishers apologise for any inadvertent omissions.

Text © 2004, Hannah Mortimer
© 2004, Scholastic Ltd

Designed using Adobe InDesign

Published by Scholastic Ltd, Villiers House,
Clarendon Avenue, Leamington Spa, Warwickshire CV32 5PR

Visit our website at www.scholastic.co.uk

Printed by Bell and Bain Ltd, Glasgow

1 2 3 4 5 6 7 8 9 0   4 5 6 7 8 9 0 1 2 3

British Library Cataloguing-in-Publication Data A catalogue record for this book is available from the British Library.

ISBN 0 439 971446

The essential A–Z guide to special needs

5 INTRODUCTION
9 Aggression
10 Allergy
11 Asthma
12 Attachment
13 Attention difficulties and AD/HD
14 Autistic spectrum difficulties

15 Behaviour Difficulties
16 Bereavement

17 Cancer and leukaemia
18 Cerebral palsy
19 Child development centre
20 Child Protection
21 Code of Practice for SEN
22 Cystic fibrosis

23 Developmental Delay
24 Diabetes
25 Disability Act
26 Down's syndrome
27 Dyspraxia

28 Early Years Action
29 Early Years Action Plus
30 Eczema
31 Emotional difficulties
32 Emotional literacy
33 Equal opportunities

34 Family breakdown
35 Family therapy

36 Hearing Impairment
37 HIV/AIDS

38 IEP
39 Inclusion
40 Independence training

CONTENTS · CONTENTS · CONTENTS · CONTENTS · CONTENTS

41 Learning difficulties

42 Medical difficulties
43 Meningitis
44 Multiple difficulties

45 Parent supporters
46 Physical difficulties
47 Play therapy

48 Self-esteem
49 Semantic pragmatic difficulties
50 SEN
51 SENCO
52 SEN policy
53 Separation anxiety
54 Specific learning difficulties (including dyslexia)
55 Speech and language difficulties
56 Spina bifida and hydrocephalus
57 Stammering
58 Statement of SEN

59 Tantrums
60 Toilet training
61 Trauma

62 Visual impairment

63 USEFUL CONTACTS

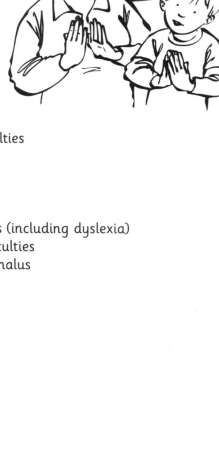

INTRODUCTION

This book is a special educational needs dictionary, providing practitioners with all the information they will need on behavioural and emotional problems, medical conditions, legal requirements and SEN terms.

The aims of the series

A revised Code of Practice for the identification and assessment of special educational needs has been published by the DfES. There are also new guidelines for providing day care, for including children with disabilities and for removing barriers to achievement. This series aims to provide suggestions to early years practitioners on how to meet and monitor special educational needs (SEN) under the new guidelines. In addition, the QCA Early Learning Goals emphasise the key role that early years educators play in identifying needs and responding quickly to them.

Within this *Special Needs in the Early Years* series, there are already seven books on helping children with most kinds of special need:
- autistic spectrum difficulties
- behavioural and emotional difficulties
- learning difficulties
- medical difficulties
- physical and co-ordination difficulties
- sensory difficulties
- speech and language difficulties.

In addition, an eighth book, the *Special Needs Handbook*, provides general information to help you meet all the special educational needs in your setting. A further two books now complement this series:
- *SEN Co-ordinator's Handbook* – for supporting colleagues in early years settings
- *The Essential A–Z Guide to Special Needs* – providing basic information for early years staff.

Who this book is for

First and foremost, this book is for early years educators who work on a daily basis with the children. It is also for SENCOs, Area SENCOs and managers to use with all the early years staff they work with. Additionally, it will be a useful reference for parents, carers, support groups and childminders.

Each registered setting is required to appoint a special educational needs co-ordinator (or 'SENCO') who will act as the contact point for all SEN matters. Many SENCOs are also taking on a new role in ensuring equal opportunities within their settings. There are now requirements for SENCOs to support their colleagues in meeting

SEN in their settings. This is because it is the responsibility of *each staff member* to support children who have SEN and not just the SENCO. This A–Z fact book will help SENCOs provide colleagues with the general information they need about conditions, terms, issues and guidelines, all in one place for easy reference.

SENCOs are busy people and cannot always be present when a member of staff needs quick and basic information. This book will provide staff with their first point of reference for understanding SEN and will be helpful to have close at hand in a busy nursery or classroom. The SENCO should then be able to provide further information and detail as needed, leaning on the other books in this series and particularly the *SENCO Handbook*.

How to use the book

You are not expected to be an expert on SEN. You are already developing your expertise in individual children, how they learn and play, their strengths and their weaknesses. This book provides you with the very basics, so that you can be familiar enough with the terminology and issues to be able to ask the right questions and talk confidently with parents and carers. The book covers 54 frequently used terms, approaches or conditions associated with special educational needs, arranged in alphabetical order with each one on a separate page. You can dip into the book for quick reference, or you can skim through these easy-to-read pages to provide yourself with a basic level of knowledge.

On each page, you will find a few basic facts that will be helpful for you to know. There might be a definition of a certain term or a description of a certain condition. This is followed by a section on 'How to help', which lists the essentials of what it actually means for you and your practice. A section is included on working with parents and on making links with other relevant professionals or agencies. There are also pointers for 'Finding out more', either from an organisation or through reading more about the subject. At the end of the book, there is a list of useful contacts including voluntary organisations and suppliers of resources. You will find further lists in the other books within the *Special Needs in the Early Years* series.

The SEN Code of Practice

All registered early years settings are required to 'have regard to' the SEN Code of Practice. This is a guide for school governors, registered early years providers and local education authorities, about the practical help they can give to children with special educational needs. It recommends that schools and early years providers should identify children's needs and take action to meet those needs as early as possible, working with parents. The aim is to enable all pupils with SEN to reach their full potential, to be included fully in their school communities and to make a successful transition to adulthood. The Code gives guidance to schools and early years providers, but it does not tell them what they must do in every case. It is recognised that good practice can take many forms and early years providers are encouraged to adopt a flexible and a graduated

response to the SEN of individual children. This approach recognises that there is a continuum of SEN and, where necessary, brings increasing specialist expertise on board if the child is experiencing continuing difficulties. Once a child's SEN have been identified, the providers should intervene through Early Years Action. This intervention is co-ordinated by one person within the setting who has been designated as the SEN link person, the 'SENCO'. However, each adult in the setting shares the responsibility of intervening to support the child.

When reviewing the child's progress and the help they are receiving, the provider might decide to seek alternative approaches to learning through the support of the outside support services. These interventions are known as 'Early Years Action Plus'.

Early Years Action Plus is characterised by the involvement of specialists from outside the setting. For a very few children, the help provided by Early Years Action Plus will still not be sufficient to ensure satisfactory progress. The provider, external professionals and parents may then decide to ask the local education authority (LEA) to consider carrying out a statutory assessment of the child's SEN.

Providing education and care

Registered early years providers are also expected to deliver this broad and balanced curriculum across six Areas of Learning as defined in the Early Learning Goals and the *Curriculum Guidance for the Foundation Stage* (QCA). Defining a set of Early Learning Goals, which most children will have attained by the end of the Foundation Stage (the end of their Reception year), has helped to ensure that nursery education is of good quality and a sound preparation for later schooling. In order to ensure this, registered early years providers are required to have their educational provision inspected regularly. One of the areas inspected is how effectively staff identify, support and monitor the needs of the children with SEN in the setting.

The 'Full Day Care Standards' (ref DfES 0488/2001, available online at www.surestart.gov.uk) contains guidance on the standards that settings should aim for in all aspects of childcare including meeting SEN and the provision of equal opportunities. Quite often, it is the SENCO in the setting who is also given the role of being the contact person for equal opportunities. That is why you will find sections in this book about equal opportunities and inclusion as well as SEN issues and conditions.

Developing inclusive practice

'Inclusion' is the practice of including all children together in a setting. All children should participate fully in all the regular routines and activities of the classroom or playroom, though these might need to be modified to meet individual children's goals and objectives. There seem to be certain common features that promote inclusion.

● There is usually careful joint-planning. For example, if there is special support for a child, how will it be used? Will the child still have access to the full range of adults, children and activities?

● Staff use educational labels rather than categories or medical labels (such as 'a child who has epilepsy' rather than 'an epileptic' or 'a child who has SEN' rather than 'an SEN child').

● Early years staff provide good role models for the children because of their positive expectations and the way they respect each child.

● Special attention is given to improving children's access and communication skills.

● Teaching strategies are developed which enable *all* children to participate and to learn.

● Individual approaches are planned which draw on pupils' earlier experiences, set high expectations, and encourage mutual peer help and support.

● There is a flexible use of support to promote joining in and inclusion rather than to create barriers and exclusion.

Trying a range of approaches

In an inclusive approach, your task becomes one of making the Foundation Stage curriculum accessible to all. The two main ways in which you can set out to achieve this is by making sure that the curriculum you offer is both *inclusive* (for everybody) and *differentiated* (to the needs of the child with SEN). Having 'special' activities for 'special' children and buying plenty of 'special needs' equipment does not help the development of inclusive services. Often, an activity can be changed in some way rather than excluding certain children from it because they cannot 'fit in' with it. Flexible approaches and adaptable routines make this easier. Outdoor play areas need to contain quiet, sheltered spaces as well as busy active areas. Indoors, tables and equipment need to be at adjustable heights and floor spaces should be comfortable and safe to play on. Acoustics can be softened with soft surfaces, cushions, carpets and curtains, making it easier for everyone to hear clearly. Story times can be kept concrete by using props and visual aids. Communication can be enhanced by making sure that all adults are familiar with any language or communication system used by the children. Children can also have a communication book showing how they make their needs known. Making more use of colours, textures and smells can encourage different senses. Early years practitioners can look for ways of making their tools and equipment easy to handle by all children. Throughout the curriculum, practitioners can look out for materials, pictures and books that portray positive images of disabled people and special needs.

There is an overlap between disability, special educational needs and significant medical difficulties, and this is why you will find pages on all of these. Not all children who are disabled (for example, have a limb missing) or who have a medical condition (such as severe eczema) will have special educational needs. However, it is helpful if you can understand all of these conditions so that you can make sure each child is fully included in your setting.

Aggression

What you need to know
● Some children find it hard to play alongside other children without biting, kicking or hitting them. There are many different reasons for this and you cannot make assumptions.
● Sometimes these children might catch your eye first before behaving aggressively. This suggests that they are seeking attention.
● Some might seem constantly angry or frustrated because they find it hard to speak clearly, to understand or to hear.
● Others love rough-and-tumble play, but tend to become over-boisterous and aggressive.
● For others still, the aggressive behaviour might be linked to their experiences of being parented or to past events in their lives.
● There are some children who would love to make friends, but who lack social skills and end up being too physical with other children.

How to help
● Sit down with colleagues and decide what you mean when you say the child is being aggressive. What is the child actually doing that everyone can observe?
● Decide why you feel a child is being aggressive. You can do this by observing the child carefully.
● Try a 'fly-on-the-wall' observation where you record what the child does over an hour or so. Ask colleagues to deal with all incidents in their usual way.
● Alternatively, you can use an 'ABC' chart, recording difficult times by listing what led up to the incident (the antecedent), what the child actually did (the behaviour), and what happened as a result (the consequence).
● You can then plan an intervention that involves changing the antecedent or the consequence and make sure that all your colleagues follow the same approach.
● This might involve avoiding certain difficult times, perhaps by making sure that an adult plays near the child whenever a certain other child is present.
● It might involve giving more attention to the child who is hurt and also praising the children when they are playing in a friendly way.
● You will need to give short, clear rules and intervene in a consistent way.

Finding out more
Managing Children's Behaviour from the *Early Years Training and Management* series by Hannah Mortimer (Scholastic).

WORKING WITH CARERS
● Talk with parents and carers about whether the child's behaviour is the same at home. What do they do that helps?

MAKING LINKS
● Find out from the local education authority who your early years/behaviour support teacher is, for general advice and training.

Allergy

What you need to know

● Some children react to certain substances by producing a rash, runny nose and sore eyes, or developing breathing difficulties or changed behaviour. This is due to an altered immune response in their bodies called an allergic reaction.

● The sorts of substances that children with allergies react to range widely. They might be things a child has inhaled, touched or taken into their bodies, such as pollen, dust mites, animals, penicillin, nuts (such as peanuts), foods, latex or certain chemicals.

● An allergic condition can be very mild or extremely serious and life-threatening, as when a child goes into 'anaphylactic shock' and emergency help is needed immediately. The severity of the condition depends on the individual child and the particular reaction they produce in response to the allergen.

● Allergic reactions might be delayed or might develop very quickly and obviously.

● These children are not infectious and an allergy cannot be 'caught'.

How to help

● Ask parents/carers routinely about any allergies their child has when they first join your setting.

● Find out what this means for the child and for you. How serious is the reaction? What are the signs you should look out for and at what stage should you take any special action? What foods or situations should be avoided? Look for a 'common sense' balance between keeping early years experiences as normal as possible yet taking reasonable precautions to ensure that the child remains comfortable and safe.

● Keep an eye on the environment outside your setting, so that you can close windows if the traffic pollution is particularly bad or the pollen count high.

● If a child is very uncomfortable, stay calm, reassure and distract them while you take any necessary action.

● Make sure that you are absolutely certain about the ingredients of the food you provide; for some children it is essential that they do not have even the smallest trace of an allergen such as a nut.

Finding out more

The Anaphylaxis Campaign produces guidance for carers of pre-school children. Send an sae to PO Box 149, Fleet, Hampshire GU13 9XU for information, or contact via the website, www.anaphylaxis.org.uk.

WORKING WITH CARERS

● For children who have marked symptoms, or for those whose allergies are still being assessed, keep a diary to share with parents and carers about what led up to a reaction, what the reaction was, and what happened as a result. This is useful for carers to share with doctors.

MAKING LINKS

● Contact your local health visitor for general advice about management of a child's allergies.

Asthma

What you need to know
● Children with asthma have a condition in which they cough, wheeze, have a tight chest and get short of breath.
● This is because their airways are almost always inflamed and sensitive. These airways react badly when the child has a cold or comes into contact with an asthma 'trigger'.
● Common asthma triggers include colds, viral infections, pollen, cigarette smoke, house-dust mites, furry or feathered pets, exercise, air pollution and stress.
● Children whose asthma has been diagnosed by a doctor will need to take a dose of their prescribed reliever medication when they have symptoms. This is usually given by inhaler. Some children need to use a preventer inhaler each day as well.
● Asthma symptoms can be very mild for some children, and extremely severe for others.

How to help
● Keep a diary record for any child who has asthma so that you can identify any triggers in your setting. Record the child's symptoms and what you think might have set them off.
● Keep any inhalers in a safe place, clearly marked with the child's name, and make sure you take them on any trips. Have a spare available in the setting if it is in frequent use.
● Make sure that a child's reliever inhaler is always at hand and is used as soon as the child starts to cough, wheeze and become short of breath. Parents/carers may also advise you to use it *before* physical activity or other events that might trigger an attack.
● Stay calm and reassure the child. Reliever inhalers usually work quickly to relax the muscles. Do not put your arm around the child's shoulders as this can restrict breathing.
● Encourage the child to breathe slowly and deeply by breathing with them. As soon as the attack is over, help the child return to their normal activities.
● If the medication does not work after five to ten minutes, if the child is too distressed to talk, or if you are worried about their condition, call an ambulance. Parents or carers can tell you what would constitute an emergency in their child's case.
● Help the child avoid making contact with known triggers as far as you are able. This might involve keeping your soft surfaces dust-free, keeping the child away from furry pets, and taking general common-sense precautions against spreading coughs and colds.

Finding out more
The National Asthma Campaign publishes various helpful documents write to: Providence House, Providence Place, London N1 0NT (Tel: 020 7226 2260), or visit their website at www.asthma.org.uk.

WORKING WITH CARERS
● When the child joins your group, talk to parents or carers about what seem to be the triggers for their child's asthma and what steps you should take.
● Find out from parents how the inhaler works and what sort of help you should provide.
● Share any asthma diary daily.

MAKING LINKS
● Contact your local health visitor for general advice on coping with asthma.

SPECIAL NEEDS in the early years

Attachment

What you need to know

● 'Attachment Theory' argues that children develop a style of relating to important attachment figures in their lives, which secures for them the best parenting available under the circumstances.

● The patterns of attachment remain remarkably consistent over time until the child is about six, and so can be observed, identified and worked with by specialists.

● Where there are difficulties in attachment, parents/carers may find that their young child is difficult to control, extremely angry and aggressive, or highly anxious and 'clingy'.

● Where attachment is working securely right from the start, an infant's cries and demands will be met reliably with sensitivity and warmth by the parent or carer, and the growing child develops in confidence and independence.

● If a parent is unresponsive or rejecting of their cries of distress, that child may act as if they are independent long before they are emotionally ready to be. They may pay little attention when their parent leaves them at nursery, and seldom look at their parent or try to involve them in their play. This is known as a pattern of 'anxious-avoidant' attachment.

● If a parent is inconsistent in their responses, perhaps because of periods of depression or frequent absences, the child learns to cry or shout louder with their demands, producing a pattern of 'ambivalent' attachment.

How to help

● These children settle better if given 'secure attachment figures' to relate to in the nursery or playgroup. This might be an interested key worker who can support, offer consistency of handling, and be there to reassure and to encourage.

● Try to identify those children who have low self-esteem (see page 48) and need more than the usual level of reassurance and praise. These are the children who need added support and encouragement in order to help them feel that they are successful in their play, their learning and their relationships.

Finding out more

Send for a catalogue of the 'Understanding Childhood' leaflets from The Child Psychotherapy Trust, Star House, 104–108 Grafton Road, London NW5 4BD or visit their website at: www.childpsychotherapytrust.org.uk

WORKING WITH CARERS

Understanding about attachments does not mean that you should tell a parent or carer that their child 'has an attachment difficulty'. This would be totally unhelpful. However, it does help you to focus on planning activities to help parents and children tune into each other and share pleasure and fun.

MAKING LINKS

● The local health visitor or GP might consider referring the family to the local 'CAMHS' (mental health) support team. Most Sure Start schemes also work with families to improve attachments.

Attention difficulties and AD/HD

What you need to know

● Some children have attention difficulties that are *greater than for other children their age*. This is because they have a physiological difference in their brains controlling their arousal system. It can be helped through careful behaviour management and also sometimes through medication (such as Ritalin).

● In the early years, these children may or may not have been diagnosed as having 'attention deficit/hyperactivity disorder' (AD/HD) and there are two reasons for this.

● Firstly, most children in the early years are highly active at least some of the time – most settle down as their concentration develops.

● Secondly, medication should not be prescribed until the child is old enough to have a say in how the medicine makes them feel – usually about the age of six. This is because the side effects can be very unpleasant and can also suppress appetite.

● It makes more sense for you to identify if a child has difficulties in attention and concentration and plan the best approaches to help. You do not need a diagnosis to do that.

How to help

● Children with short attention spans will benefit from clear routines and structures so that they know what is going to happen and when.

● 'Sandwich' short periods of sustained concentration and effort with periods of time when the child can be more active or have free choice in their play. Give very strong encouragement and praise to keep this fun, attention-getting and motivating for the child.

● Break tasks down into simpler steps so that a child with a short attention span can still play and learn from them.

● Find a distraction-free space for activities that require sustained concentration, looking or listening, and work in smaller groups.

● Make sure you have eye contact before speaking to the child and use their name and a touch to gain attention. Be prepared to give reminders constantly.

● Give very clear, short and concrete directions, showing the child what to do as well as telling.

Finding out more

Supporting Children with AD/HD and Attention Difficulties in the Early Years by Hannah Mortimer (QEd Publications).

WORKING WITH CARERS
● Explain to parents and carers that they are likely to find themselves very busy for a while and offer them advice and support during what might be a trying time for them.

MAKING LINKS
● Most NHS Trusts have a service for identifying and supporting children with AD/HD. The health visitor is likely to know more.

Autistic spectrum difficulties

What you need to know

● Some children appear indifferent to other people and behave as if they are 'in a world of their own'. They might have been diagnosed as having 'autism', 'autistic features' or 'Asperger's syndrome'. All these conditions have some overlap.

● These children may tend not to play with other children and may join in with activities only if an adult insists and assists.

● They may have very little language, they may echo what is said to them, or they may talk a lot about topics of great interest to them.

● Sometimes, they may become absorbed in arranging toys in a certain way, collecting certain objects, or spinning or turning toys repeatedly to watch them move.

● Their eye contact may be very poor and they may be unable to play imaginatively, unless it is in a very stereotyped way.

● Their behaviour may be bizarre or very fearful, especially if familiar routines are disturbed or if they feel stressed.

How to help

● Start by helping the child feel settled when playing one-to-one with a key worker. Gradually involve one or more other children in the play, but stay close to support and assist.

● Play turn-taking games, for example blowing bubbles for the child to burst, or rolling a musical ball to and fro. The idea here is that the child will begin to see your company as useful and fun.

● Try to keep to a familiar and structured routine. Take a series of photographs of a typical session and show the child these to illustrate what is happening next.

● Provide a simple commentary about what the child is doing, for example: 'Tom is *painting*.'

● Give plenty of encouragement whenever the child communicates with you, whether by voice or through actions.

● Show interest in the child's intense interests but introduce new things too. Support the child's choice of activities, but distract the child if they become too absorbed or obsessed with them.

● Provide a quiet 'safe base' where the child can go if they feel 'over-loaded' or stressed. Provide some favourite music or activity there so the child can relax.

Finding out more

The National Autistic Society provides support and advice for carers and professionals. You can contact them at: 393, City Road, London EC1V 1NG. Tel: 0870 600 85 85, or visit their website at www.nas.org.uk.

WORKING WITH CARERS
● Photographs of daily routines can be used at home as well to help children understand what is happening when.

MAKING LINKS
● Many LEA support services now have a 'specialist autism team' – contact the local education department for information.

Behaviour difficulties

What you need to know

● If a child has had time to settle with you and is not responding to your encouragement and boundary setting despite all your usual approaches, then you might consider talking to parents/carers about employing approaches that are additional to or different from the usual.

● These are the children who you would describe as having 'behavioural difficulties', who would benefit from being on your SEN records and having a within-setting individual behaviour plan.

● There are four main criteria for helping you to decide that a behaviour is abnormal or problematic:

'fixation': a behaviour has continued beyond the age where it might be considered appropriate

'regression': a behaviour might have been achieved successfully at an appropriate age and the child then reverts back to behaviour characteristic of a younger age

'failure to display': a behaviour that should have developed by a particular age, has not done so

'exaggeration': a normal behaviour, such as a burst of temper, might become exaggerated into a full-blown temper tantrum in which other children get hurt.

How to help

● Always talk in terms of 'problem behaviour' rather than 'problem children' since most potential for change lies in how everyone else *manages* that behaviour.

● Start by standing back and observing how a child is behaving. Record clearly what they do over a half-hour, warning other colleagues to manage the behaviour using the same techniques as they would usually.

● Work out from your observations what behaviour you would wish to change, what led up to the difficult moment and what the consequences were. This is called an 'ABC' observation (antecedent, behaviour, consequence).

● From this, work out how you can change the 'A', the 'B' or the 'C'.

● You might be able to avoid certain situations altogether for a while, teach or encourage another more appropriate behaviour or distract the child with something else to do

● Use strong praise and rewards when the child is behaving appropriately and make sure that any sanctions you use are not rewarding in themselves – for example, sitting in the staff room where the biscuits are!

Finding out more

Managing Children's Behaviour from the Early Years Training and Management series by Hannah Mortimer (Scholastic).

WORKING WITH CARERS
● Always discuss behavioural difficulties with parents and carers. Find a way to word this constructively – 'What do you find works best at home?'

MAKING LINKS
● Talk with your SENCO or Area SENCO for ideas on behaviour management and see page 38 to help you write your individual behaviour/education plan.

SPECIAL NEEDS in the early years

Bereavement

What you need to know

● Forty thousand families worldwide experience the death of a child each day.

● Most families will face bereavement following the death of a relative at some time and young children may come across death early in their lives.

● Young children find it hard to accept the permanence of death. Dealing with the death of a family pet sometimes helps with this.

How to help

● When someone in the family of a child attending your setting dies, try not to let your embarrassment and fear of not knowing what to say get in the way of speaking to that family.

● Avoid giving direct advice and platitudes (for example, 'Time will heal' or, 'You're taking it so well'), but be sensitive to what practical help you can give. Perhaps you can provide additional support to siblings or friends in your setting who are dealing with grief in their own, personal ways.

● Be there to listen. If one of the children has died, find happy memories to share, and continue to talk about the child even after those first raw days.

● Do give extra attention to siblings or friends, who will be feeling confused and sad just when the adults around them may not have the time or emotional resources to comfort them.

● Talk about what has happened in clear, absolute terms, and play alongside the child, providing opportunities for them to act out some of their feelings.

● The other children too will want to talk about things. Do not be put off if the children seem almost callous in their response. The news is usually taken at a practical level with concerns like, 'Who will his mum collect from nursery now?' or, 'Who will get his bike?'

● Try to avoid using expressions that will confuse the children. If you talk of death being 'like going to sleep for ever', you can leave children very frightened about what will happen if they allow themselves to fall asleep at night.

Finding out more

The Child Bereavement Trust can be contacted at: Aston House, West Wycombe, High Wycombe, Buckinghamshire. HP14 3AG. Send for their information pack. Alternatively, visit their website at www.childbereavement.org.uk, for information, advice and support. Barnardo's 'Memory Store' and 'Memory Book' are designed for children facing separation, loss and bereavement, and are available from Barnardo's Child Care Publications, Barnardo's Trading Estate, Paycocke Road, Basildon, Essex, SS14 3DR, www.barnardos.org.uk.

WORKING WITH CARERS

● Do encourage the family to take things steadily and not try to do too much at once. They may need continual reassurance that what they did was right and best for their child.

● Siblings may need reassurance too, so that they do not feel they caused, or could have prevented, the death in some way.

MAKING LINKS

● Most hospital paediatric departments have a specialist nurse who helps with bereavement counselling and advice.

Cancer and leukaemia

What you need to know

- In a cancer, certain cells multiply too quickly. Sometimes a tumour is formed, perhaps in the brain or the bowel.
- It is usually adults who are affected, but some cancers do affect children and the most common is leukaemia.
- Leukaemia is a rare form of cancer affecting the white blood cells. Children become anaemic, their blood does not clot properly and they cannot fight infections well. So the first symptoms are increased bruising, infection and tiredness. You might also see recurrent nosebleeds, a purplish rash and the child might complain that their joints are painful.
- The outlook for children with leukaemia is much better than it used to be, with more than half being completely cured. However, the child might need to spend considerable time in hospital or receiving treatment.
- Treatments vary greatly depending on the patient and the cancer. The most common involve strong drugs or radiotherapy. Nowadays, hospitals are much better at controlling unpleasant side effects.
- These children are likely to need hospital check-ups for several years in case there is a return of the cancer.

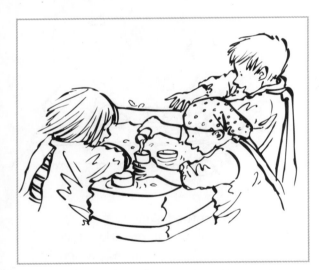

How to help

- If you are worried about a child's symptoms, have a quiet word with the parents, carers or health visitor so that the child can be medically checked. Make sure you do not alarm the parents/carers, or the child, with your reasons.
- Look for ways of keeping your links with a child who is in hospital. You will find plenty of ideas for achieving this in another book in the *Special Needs in the Early Years* series, entitled: *Medical Difficulties* (Hannah Mortimer, Scholastic).

Finding out more

The organisation Sargent Cancer Care for Children is based at Griffin House, 161 Hammersmith Road, London W6 8SG and provides support and information for families and professionals. Send off to this address for information, or visit their website, www.sargent.org.

WORKING WITH CARERS

- If a cancer or leukaemia has been diagnosed, keep closely in touch with the family and help to maintain the morale of family, siblings and friends while the child is away.
- When a child is being treated or is still convalescing, warn parents/carers if there are any infectious diseases in the setting, such as chicken pox.

MAKING LINKS

- Ask carers for the name of the child's specialist cancer nurse, so that you can ask how you can best support the child and family over this time.

SPECIAL NEEDS
C
in the early years

WORKING WITH CARERS

● Seating, posture and positioning are vitally important to prevent problems in bones later on. You will need to talk to parents and carers about the correct ways to physically handle the child, and hopefully meet with the physiotherapist and occupational therapist.

MAKING LINKS

● It should be possible for you to borrow the correct table, chair or buggy from the hospital, Social Services or through the parents/carers.

● The therapists will also be able to help you play with the child in a way that makes the best use of their movements. Find out just what you need to do to cope with nappies or toilet routines, feeding, drinking, and how much help is required with dressing and undressing.

Cerebral palsy

What you need to know

● About 1,500 babies are born with or develop cerebral palsy every year in Britain. It is caused when part of the child's brain is not working properly, so that body movements cannot be co-ordinated by the brain.

● Sometimes this brain injury is caused by an early infection during pregnancy, sometimes from a bleed in the brain in very premature babies, sometimes from a loss of oxygen to the brain, or sometimes because the brain has not developed normally. This leads to the messages from brain to muscles and back again becoming jumbled.

● Cerebral palsy is not a degenerative illness, but a condition that can be worked on with therapy and encouragement so that the child is affected as little as possible.

● Symptoms might be very slight or so severe that the child needs help in every day-to-day task. Movements may be slow and awkward, floppy or stiff, poorly controlled, and sometimes unwanted.

● You must never assume that because children have considerable physical difficulties, they will also be slow in their thinking and intelligence.

How to help

● Clearly, these children will not have had the same learning experiences as children without a physical difficulty, so here is where your setting can begin to redress the balance.

● Make sure that the early years curriculum you provide is fully accessible to the child by making all the reasonable adjustments needed both in your physical spaces and in the activities you plan.

● Think about each play activity and how you can involve a child who has physical difficulties. Perhaps an activity can be rearranged at floor level. Perhaps all the children can sit at the water tray.

● Keep floor spaces clear from obstacles and child-friendly for non-ambulant children.

Finding out more

The organisation SCOPE 6 Market Road, London N7 9PW runs a cerebral palsy helpline: telephone free on 0800 800 3333. You can also visit their website, www.scope.org.uk.

Child development centre

What you need to know

● Early years professionals who serve children with disabilities, and the families of those children, have been urged to work more closely together for many years now.

● One way they can do this is to provide assessment within multidisciplinary teams, working together with the parents and carers to 'discover' the child's needs and negotiate the best support.

● The Court Report (1976) led to the setting up of multidisciplinary teams to provide diagnosis, assessment, treatment and education for children with 'handicaps' as they were then termed.

● These teams were made up of paediatricians, nursing officers, social workers, therapists, psychologists and teachers who were based in 'child development centres' in each Health Area.

● Child development centres tend to work with young children where there are concerns about one or more aspect of development.

● Children and families are offered diagnosis and multidisciplinary assessment of congenital and acquired disabilities and learning difficulties, with treatment and intervention.

● Advice, counselling and support are available to parents, carers and families, and useful information on statutory and voluntary services is also provided.

● These centres are also able to help with advice on the children's special educational needs and each professional involved usually contributes to the statutory assessment and statementing procedure.

● Nowadays, there is a move towards supporting children and their families in their own homes and communities wherever possible, although the child development centres have remained as bases for professional teams and for multidisciplinary assessment.

How to help

● If one of the children is due to attend a child development centre, provide parents and carers with a brief report on how their child is doing in your setting. Emphasise the child's strengths and successes and also those areas where they need help. Finally, make it clear what further information *you* need in order support the child.

● Most children who are assessed at a child development centre will go on to have their progress reviewed there. It might be possible for the SENCO to attend this review meeting and share progress and any concerns.

Finding out more

Find out where your nearest child development centre is from the health visitor or Community Health Council. Send for a pamphlet to add to your carers' resources.

WORKING WITH CARERS

● Use parents and carers as a go-between so that you can work in conjunction with the centre, for example by using diaries that go between home, setting and centre.

MAKING LINKS

● Offer an invitation to professionals involved to visit you, and seek their advice when you need it.

Child protection

What you need to know

● Everyone who comes into contact with children on a regular basis has a duty to safeguard and promote the welfare of children.
● Each setting should have a copy of the local procedures and also have provided training in 'child protection' to its staff.
● It is up to each individual to make sure they are aware of the child protection procedures in that setting and area.
● Social services involvement has increased since the Children Act 1989 and you might have to work with a social worker, providing information about a child during a child protection enquiry or taking part in a multi-agency assessment. Social services can also give you some general advice.

● If you are worried that a child is being abused, you must refer these concerns to social services or the police, usually through the manager/Head/SENCO or the person who is your designated contact for child protection.
● Child abuse can take different forms: physical (as in marks, bruises and injuries), sexual (perhaps the child has disclosed some information to you), emotional abuse, or neglect (perhaps the child is failing to thrive).

How to help

● Always discuss concerns with a manager or designated contact.
● Always keep records of incidents – what was said, what you did and when the incident occurred.
● Always be ready to listen to the child.
● Do not use leading questions that might later distort evidence.
● Always make sure that you are not putting yourself in a vulnerable position with a child that might lead to allegations against your own behaviour.
● The protection of the child is absolutely paramount.
● If you make a referral by telephone, always confirm it in writing within 48 hours.

Finding out more

Send for the booklet: 'What To Do If You're Worried a Child is Being Abused' (ref. 31815) from the Department of Health Publications. Tel: 020 7210 4850. This is also available from www.publications.doh.gov.uk/safeguardingchildren.

WORKING WITH CARERS
● If you make a referral to social services or police, agree with that agency what the child and parents/carers will be told, by whom and when.

MAKING LINKS
● Your local Social Services Department will provide you with advice or take action if you are concerned – contact the local duty officer.

Code of Practice for SEN

What you need to know

● The SEN Code of Practice was revised in 2002 and all early years settings registered to receive funding from their LEA are required to have regard to its advice and guidance.

● It provides you with information on how to identify, assess, intervene and monitor children with special educational needs in your setting.

● Instead of the five-stage approach of the 'old' Code of Practice, there is now a graded approach to identifying and meeting SEN. This is in three phases:

Early Years Action, where the setting assesses and meets the SEN (see page 28)
Early Years Action Plus, where you bring on board outside professional help (see page 29)
Statemented provision, where the LEA determines and monitors the SEN (see page 58)

● Individual education plans (IEPs) should be a key feature of planning for any SEN in your group (see page 38).
● There is also a move towards greater inclusion (see page 39) and this has been further strengthened by the SEN Disability Act (see page 25).

How to help

● Ask your SENCO to provide you with basic training in the *Code* so that you are aware of what it means for your practice.
● If you feel that a child may have special needs, then the SENCO should be able to help you assess the child's difficulties, plan interventions and work with parents and carers to ensure the child makes reasonable progress in spite of their needs.
● It is each early years worker's responsibility to identify and meet special educational needs – not just the SENCO's – but you will need the support and advice of the SENCO or other professionals to do this.
● Contact the local Early Years Support Service for information on SEN training.

Finding out more

Copies of the Code can be obtained from DfES Publications at: PO Box 5050, Sherwood Park, Annesley, Nottinghamshire NG15 0DJ (email: dfes@prolog.uk.com), quoting reference DfES 581/2001. Visit the DfES website, www.dfes.gov.uk, for materials and information. *Removing Barriers to Achievement: The Government's Strategy for SEN* is available from the DfES and can be accessed at www.teachernet.gov.uk/wholeschool/sen/senstrategy.

WORKING WITH CARERS
● There should be a greater involvement of parents and carers who should now have more rights and wider choices.

MAKING LINKS
● You may find yourself working with members of the early years/SEN support team for your area, perhaps alongside a support teacher, Portage worker or psychologist. They can provide advice on your IEP, approaches and monitoring.

Cystic fibrosis

What you need to know

● Some children are born with a condition called cystic fibrosis. It affects about one in 2,000 children.

● For these children, the mucous glands produce abnormally thick, sticky mucus and their sweat glands produce excess salt.

● Though their lungs will have been normal at birth, each time they have an infection this sticky mucus collects in the lungs and blocks airways causing further damage.

● Their pancreas will be affected too. The small channels that normally allow enzymes to flow into the intestine become blocked leading to cysts. That is why these children need to take digestive enzymes orally at mealtimes.

● Children with cystic fibrosis have daily physiotherapy to help drain the mucus from various parts of the lungs.

How to help

● Make sure the child leads as normal a life as possible. Apart from having physiotherapy, taking enzymes and doing exercise every day, the child should be able to do the same as most other children their age. Your task is to make them feel like everyone else.

● On hot days, you may need to remind the child to take extra salt. Ask parents and carers what to do and when.

● If you are together at mealtimes, then the child will need to take regular enzymes. If they do not, they will begin to feel tired, get stomach-ache, and need to go to the toilet a lot.

● Expect the child to be absent from time to time for medical check-ups or when they are fighting infections.

● Have a quiet area that the child can settle into if they are feeling tired or unwell.

● Encourage physical exercise; again, parents/carers will tell you how much exercise their child should be getting each day. Exercise helps the lungs to stay fitter.

● Keep parents/carers informed of any infections going around. Though most children with cystic fibrosis are encouraged to keep attending, additional antibiotics might be needed.

Finding out more

The Cystic Fibrosis Trust can be contacted at: 11 London Road, Bromley BR1 1BY. (Tel: 020 8464 7211) or via their website, www.cftrust.org.uk.

WORKING WITH CARERS

● Talk with parents and carers to make sure that you know everything you need to about their child's condition. Children may be affected differently, so this information is important to have.

MAKING LINKS

● Ask parents/carers to introduce you to their child's physiotherapist, so that you can make sure you are doing all you should to support the child.

Developmental delay

What you need to know

● Children differ widely in the age at which they reach various developmental stages. It is quite normal to have a wide variation in your setting.

● However, some children fail to achieve their developmental milestones within the usual time range and are sometimes described as being 'delayed' in their development.

● For some children, there might be a clear cause – perhaps they have a chromosomal condition, such as Down's syndrome (see page 26), or perhaps they have not yet had the necessary early years experiences for learning and development.

● For others, there may be no known cause; it is simply that a child seems to be taking longer than other children to progress.

● Some children will eventually catch up. Others may continue to have learning difficulties. At this stage, you should provide the same amount of help.

How to help

● Keep story times and talk-about times simple by using props for the child to look at and handle.

● Emphasise key words and keep your language simple and clear.

● To fully engage the child's attention, establish eye contact before speaking.

● Show *and* tell the child what to do.

● Keep activities short and end on a successful note.

● Use praise and encouragement to make children feel successful when they are playing.

● Use a structured step-by-step approach for teaching new developmental skills, such as putting on a coat or washing hands. Help only at those moments when the child cannot manage. Encourage the child to be as independent as possible and to be proud of it.

● Use small groups and circles to encourage language and listening.

● Provide materials that make it possible for the child to participate fully (for example, chubby crayons and brushes for immature hand-holds, squeezy scissors, wooden formboard puzzles with knobs on for easy holding).

Finding out more

You will find practical information about all of these approaches in another book from this series, *Learning difficulties* by Hannah Mortimer (Scholastic).

WORKING WITH CARERS

● Maintain regular contact with parents and carers so that you can be kept in touch with any therapy goals from other professionals.

MAKING LINKS

● Contact your Area or School SENCO for information about learning support services in your area.

Diabetes

What you need to know

● Diabetes is caused when there is not enough insulin produced in the body. Insulin is a hormone responsible for glucose metabolism and it helps us to store glucose ready for when we need energy.

● There are about 15 to 20 children per 100 000 diagnosed with diabetes each year and this is increasing.

● It can start quite suddenly without there being any known reason, and it can also run in families.

● The first symptoms you might notice are excessive thirst, large amounts of urine being passed frequently, weight loss, irritability and tiredness, an unusual smell of pear drops to the breath and a reduced resistance to infections.

● It is diagnosed through a blood test and children are usually prescribed regular insulin injections to control their blood sugar level.

● Many older children give the injections to themselves and can also learn how to test their blood and urine sugar levels.

● If the child's blood sugar level falls too low, this is called a hypoglycaemia episode or a 'hypo'.

How to help

● Most parents and carers will send in any snacks that might be necessary before the child does physical exercise, such as on sports day. They might ask you to have a sugary drink on hand for their child at these times.

● Make sure the child never misses a meal or snack time.

● Look out for a 'hypo'; symptoms can vary, but include hunger, sweating, drowsiness, pallor, glazed eyes, shaking, poor concentration and irritability.

● If parents/carers need you to check sugar levels (and this has been agreed with your managers), ask them to show you how to use any special equipment.

● Let parents/carers know when there are infections in your setting; sometimes this means different insulin requirements.

● Many children who have diabetes have the condition under control and it should not affect your time together in the setting, apart from the need to look out for a sugar 'hypo'.

Finding out more

Diabetes UK is based at: 10 Queen Anne Street, London W1M 0BD (Website: www.diabetes.org.uk).

WORKING WITH CARERS

● Talk to parents or carers about their child's regime. What special diet is the child on? What signs will you see when the child's blood sugar has fallen too low and what should you do about it?

MAKING LINKS

● The local health visitor will be able to give you more information and advice if you need it.

Disability Act

What you need to know
● The Disability Discrimination Act 1995 (DDA) introduced new legal measures.
● It clarifies disabled people's rights in terms of employment, obtaining goods and services, buying or renting land or property, and transport.
● The Act was amended to cover the requirements on establishments which provide education and day care for children and this formed the Special Educational Need and Disability Act (SENDA) 2001.
● Under the Act, a disabled person has 'a physical or mental impairment, which has an effect on his or her ability to carry out normal day-to-day activities. That effect must be substantial (not trivial or minor), adverse and long-term'.
● Many children who are disabled will have SEN and many children who have SEN are likely to be disabled in some way, so there is considerable overlap.
● Settings are also required to overcome physical features that impede access to a service and from 2004 may have to make other 'reasonable adjustments' to the physical environment to overcome physical barriers to access.

● The detail of the act has still to be tested, so the practical implications for settings will become clearer over time'.

How to help
● You cannot refuse a service (such as early years education), offer a worse standard of service or offer a service on worse terms to a disabled child or person unless you can offer a 'justification'. This is called the 'less favourable treatment' duty.
● Even if you have offered justification, you will be expected to demonstrate that you are planning ahead to improve access and inclusion in the future.
● You need to plan 'reasonable adjustments' for disabled children. This might include training for personal support assistants, planning accessible activities in an accessible environment, flexibility in terms of toilet arrangements and the provision of flexible transport.

Finding out more
Get copies of the 'Highlights' information sheets numbers 186 and 187 from the National Children's Bureau, 8 Wakley Street, London, EC1V 7QE (Website: www.ncb.org.uk).

WORKING WITH CARERS
● Make sure that your admissions policy states that your setting does not discriminate against disabled pupils in education, day care or any other services it provides.

MAKING LINKS
● Contact your local council offices for information on access and disability – many now have an officer who specialises in this area, though the department might vary.

SPECIAL NEEDS in the early years

Down's syndrome

What you need to know

● The word 'syndrome' means a collection of signs and characteristics. All people with Down's syndrome have certain facial and other physical characteristics that make them appear similar.

● However, it is important to realise that there are far more differences between people with Down's syndrome than there are similarities. All children are individuals in their own right and we need to respect this.

● One baby in about 1,000 is born with Down's syndrome. It is caused by an additional chromosome in each body cell. People with Down's syndrome have 47 chromosomes instead of the usual 46. This results in the development of the growing baby in the womb becoming disrupted and altered.

● The chances of a baby being born with Down's syndrome increase with the mother's age, particularly over the age of 35. This is one of the reasons older mothers are screened during pregnancy.

● Children with Down's syndrome usually have a greater difficulty learning than the majority of children their age.

● Many children with Down's syndrome are healthy, but 40 per cent have heart problems at birth and some might need surgery. There is also a much higher risk of hearing difficulties and vision needs to be carefully monitored. In addition, there is a tendency towards more frequent infections and 'chestiness'.

How to help

● Get to know the child as an individual. Find out about their likes, dislikes, strengths and weaknesses using your usual methods of observation and assessment.

● Look carefully at your early years curriculum and in particular the Stepping Stones towards each Early Learning Goal. You may find it helpful to break these Stepping Stones down into finer stages so that you can obtain a 'baseline' or starting-point for teaching.

● Then discuss with parents and carers a reasonable goal to aim for term by term. Break this down into finer steps, making each stage rewarding and especially motivating for the child. This way you should see steady progress.

Finding out more

The Down's Syndrome Association is based at: Langdon Down Centre, 2a Langdon Park, Teddington TW11 9PS.
Tel: 020 8682 4001. Website: www.downs-syndrome.org.uk.

WORKING WITH CARERS
● Keep closely in touch with parents and carers so that you can celebrate achievements at home and in the setting and build on them. Help the child to generalise what has been learned from one situation to another.

MAKING LINKS
● Contact your local Portage Service (see under 'Useful contacts' page 63 for the address) or child development centre (see page 19) if the child is known to them. They should be able to provide further advice and support.

Dyspraxia

What you need to know

- Children whose development of motor co-ordination is impaired are sometimes described as having 'developmental co-ordination difficulties' (or 'dyspraxia').
- The diagnosis is usually only made if the impairment significantly interferes with educational progress or daily activities.
- These children appear to be clumsy in their movements. They find it hard to learn how to move and balance smoothly. They may also be poor in organising themselves, find it hard to speak clearly, and find it difficult to understand where their body is in space.
- Compared to other children of their age, these children may find it hard to dress and undress at nursery, have a poor pencil grip, find jigsaws and puzzles hard to do, and be poorly balanced when running or climbing.
- There is usually no particular cause or neurological impairment, and it is thought that dyspraxia is related to an immaturity in the brain rather than to any damage. It can therefore usually be improved with practice, with maturity and with exercises.

How to help

- Keep motor activities as fun and motivating as possible. Children with dyspraxia need lots of practice, but will soon 'opt out' if the activities are repetitive and beyond their ability.
- Repeat back unclear language clearly in order to check that you have understood and to provide a model.
- Keep activities short and end on a successful note.
- Start fine-motor tasks with large materials (such as threading cotton reels on to thick pipe-cleaners or stacking large parcels) and progress to smaller materials as skills improve (such as threading centimetre beads on to bootlaces or stacking small cubes).
- Look for motivating ways of encouraging 'clever fingers', such as musical keyboards and computer activities.
- Make sure that the chair is the right height for the child's feet to be firmly on the floor when sitting at a table.
- Use large balls to encourage looking, tracking and catching.
- Use picture symbols to encourage the child to understand what happens next in the nursery day and to help them organise themselves and plan.
- Use circle time to encourage remembering and guessing, building the child's self-esteem in any ways you can.

Finding out more

The Dyspraxia Foundation can be contacted at: 8 West Alley, Hitchin, SG5 1EG. (Helpline tel: 01462 454986, Website: www.dyspraxiafoundation.org.uk.)

WORKING WITH CARERS
- Provide ideas for developing independence skills at home (see page 40).

MAKING LINKS
- Many children with dyspraxia are helped by occupational therapists who provide exercises to improve co-ordination.

Early Years Action

What you need to know
● The SEN Code of Practice asks you to plan the curriculum so that it is accessible for all children, including those who have SEN.
● Many children's SEN will be met simply by your adapting your approaches and targeting the learning more carefully – in other words, by your taking 'Early Years Action'.
● Other children may require 'Early Years Action Plus' where an outside professional becomes involved to support and advise you all (see page 29).

How to help
● You need to have faith that the interventions you plan *can and do work*! Do not be tempted to feel that if you have identified a child's SEN then it requires an SEN expert to deal with them. You are an expert in early learning and this is precisely what the child needs to have access to.
● If you feel a child has SEN, you should gather information from your observations and assessments. You can then plan how to make the play and early learning activities more accessible to the child, by breaking them into smaller steps or making them easier. This is known as 'differentiation'.
● A good starting-point for differentiation is to look at a child's particular strengths and interests. Choose stories, for example, that are about something the child enjoys and are at a level appropriate to the child's stage of language. Include props to hold attention, emphasise meaning and allow a child to participate with more than one sense at the same time.
● All staff should work closely with the child, following the IEP (see page 38) that has been agreed. They should also observe and record the child's progress, and meet with the parents/carers and SENCO to review progress.
● All planning for the Early Learning Goals will include a degree of planning for different levels of children's ability. Within this, it might be that some children need the learning stages broken down further, and it may be necessary to give value to a smaller and less obvious learning outcome or Stepping Stone.
● You might also need to present the activities in a different way, using adapted equipment or a more structured teaching situation, perhaps led and supported by a helper.

Finding out more
There are seven other titles in this *Special Needs in the Early Years* series, which show you how to plan Early Years Action for a range of different SENs: *Autistic spectrum difficulties*; *Behavioural and Emotional Difficulties*; *Learning Difficulties*; *Medical Difficulties*; *Physical and Co-ordination Difficulties*; *Sensory Difficulties* and *Speech and Language Difficulties* (all Hannah Mortimer, Scholastic).

WORKING WITH CARERS
● Gather information from parents and carers (they know the child best!) and use this information to help your planning.
● Parents/carers must always be kept fully informed of their child's progress.

MAKING LINKS
● Each setting should have a SEN co-ordinator, or 'SENCO' (see page 51), who will develop expertise on SEN, support you all as you meet a child's needs, and be responsible for liaising with parents and carers and any other professionals.

Early Years Action Plus

What you need to know

● Some children with SEN require higher levels of support and differentiation and you might need to bring on board specialist expertise if the child is experiencing continuing difficulties – in other words, through planning 'Early Years Action Plus'.

● This does not mean that assessment should be seen as a linear process, moving from Early Years Action to Early Years Action Plus. Instead, assessment and intervention should be appropriate to a child's individual needs at any particular time, each review of the process informing and feeding on to the next.

● In practice, you might feel after several reviews that a child is still not making the progress that might be possible. In this case, you might decide to call in an outside agency for more advice, assessment and support.

● The advice from the outside professional would then become part of the IEP (see page 38).

How to help

● Usually, a request for help from outside agencies is likely to follow a decision taken by the SENCO, colleagues and parents or carers when reviewing a child's progress in the setting. Has progress been made? What do parents/carers feel? Do you need more information and advice on the child's needs from outside?

● The SENCO will be able to support you in the action you take – he/she works closely with the member of staff responsible for the child, and draws on the advice from outside specialists, for example early years support teachers, sensory support teachers, speech and language therapists and educational psychologists.

● The SENCO also ensures that the child and parents/carers are consulted and kept informed.

● One of you will need to draw up an IEP (see page 38) that incorporates the specialist advice.

● Your role will then be to ensure that the child's IEP is incorporated within your curriculum planning for the *whole* setting.

● The SENCO will also liaise with outside specialists, arrange for the child's progress to be monitored and reviewed and keep the Head of the setting informed.

Finding out more

There is a helpful book by Sue Roffey entitled *Special Needs in the Early Years: Collaboration, Communication and Coordination* (David Fulton Publishers).

WORKING WITH CARERS
● Parents and carers should always be part of the decision to refer their child to an outside agency. In most cases, they need to give their express consent.

MAKING LINKS
● Contact your Early Years Childcare and Development Partnership for information on your local support services.

Eczema

What you need to know
● Some children have a very itchy, dry, scaly, red rash on their face, their neck, their hands and in the creases of their limbs. For some children, this is widespread and can be debilitating. For others, there are just patches.
● This is called 'eczema' and is a very common allergic reaction. It tends to run in families who suffer from hay fever and asthma.

● The most common form ('atopic eczema') typically develops in the first few months and most children grow out of it by the time they are around three.
● Eczema can be triggered by foods (such as dairy products, eggs or wheat). An attack can also be set off by stress. Sometimes eczema is caused by skin irritants, such as wool, washing detergents or pet fur.

How to help
● Find out about any special diet. You may need to ask parents/ carers to send in a special snack for their child or some soya milk instead of your usual supply.
● Ask whether there is anything that their child cannot play with. For example, some find playing with clay difficult as it can dry out the skin.
● Washing hands a lot can dry them out in time so help the child dry hands thoroughly and ask parents/carers about a moisturising (or 'emollient') cream if this will help.
● Consider adding a few drops of baby oil to your water tray if this would help a particular child. Wash the toys with warm soapy water at the end of the day to remove the film.
● Do not let your concern show itself as anxiety. If a child is irritated and upset by their condition, they need you to stay calm and to distract them as far as possible.

Finding out more
Ask your local health visitor or GP surgery for pamphlets or visit the National Eczema Organisation's website, www.eczema.org.

WORKING WITH CARERS
● Find out from parents and carers whether there are known triggers for their child's eczema. It may be that you need to ensure the child avoids physical contact with pets, or that they do not wear woolly clothes next to their skin.

MAKING LINKS
● If a child with very severe eczema is due to attend your group, consider asking the health visitor or school nurse to advise you on care and any particular precautions you need to take.

Emotional difficulties

What you need to know
● Emotional difficulties in children can take many forms and can stem from many sources. It is most important to address these early in order to prevent mental health problems developing later on.
● Sometimes, children seem extremely shy and continue to cry or to be withdrawn long after you feel they should have settled with you.
● Sometimes you will have children who continue to find it very hard to separate from their parents and carers and become very distressed on arrival and at home time.
● Others cannot seem to cope with newness, with failure or with correction. They might destroy their own work or creations as if they did not matter or behave as if they were not bothered by your praise and encouragement.

How to help
● Think about the child's self-esteem (see page 48) and about ways in which you can encourage and support them. Perhaps they are feeling under pressure in some way? Can you think of anything that would help this? Can you perhaps expect a little less of them for a while, and boost their confidence as much as possible?
● If the child has difficulties separating from a parent or carer, consider whether carers, too, are anxious about their child leaving them. Children are quick to pick up feelings and carers might unwittingly be making their child worried. Encourage carers to stay calm and reassuring, arrange for them to hand their child over to one caring adult at school, and then leave. Sometimes a quick peep back through a window will reassure them that their child has in fact settled very quickly and that the fuss was all 'for their benefit'.
● If the child suddenly becomes very anxious and quiet, or behaves in a completely different way (and seems unable to tell you why), then you should talk with carers to try to get to the bottom of it. Remember the child protection procedures (see page 20).
● Encourage the child to bring a favourite cuddly toy or mascot with them if it will help them to manage better.
● Predictable routines, clear boundaries for behaviour, and familiar people in their lives generally make children feel more secure.
● Use circle-time to help all children develop self-confidence, a positive self-image and good listening and looking skills.

Finding out more
You will find more information in *Behavioural and Emotional Difficulties* by Hannah Mortimer from the series, *Special Needs in the Early Years* (Scholastic).

WORKING WITH CARERS
● You need to keep in touch with parents and carers. Any major family changes (such as separation, bereavement, even a move of house) can upset children for a long while afterwards.

MAKING LINKS
● You might find yourself working alongside colleagues from social services, family support, services for 'looked after' children or CAMHS (child and adolescent mental health service).

Emotional literacy

What you need to know
● There is now a school of thought that claims there are many different kinds of intelligence, all of which affect our abilities.
● One of these is 'emotional intelligence'. This is a type of social intelligence that involves the ability to monitor one's own and other people's emotions, to discriminate among them, and to use the information to guide one's thinking and actions.
● Emotional intelligence is seen as involving self-awareness, the ability to manage emotions, self-motivation, empathy, and relationship skills.
● In early years, you need to be aware that some children find it genuinely more difficult than others to understand social situations and handle emotions. An understanding of the child's strengths and weaknesses in personal, social and emotional development should help you plan approaches for these children.
● The term 'emotional literacy' is sometimes used to describe the work you can do with children to foster their mental health and emotional intelligence.

How to help
● Be aware of how you will know when a child is developing emotional literacy successfully. Here are some ideas.

- Make sure that you plan opportunities for the children to talk about the way they feel.
- Help the children to develop a number of words that they can use to describe feelings.
- Make sure that the children can recognise feelings in other people, such as happy, sad, angry and scared.
- Make sure that all the children enjoy playing and feel confident in it.
- Teach the children how to show friendliness and care towards each other.
- Provide the children with different ways of controlling their anger and frustration.
- Help the children to develop and use words and negotiations to solve disputes.
- Teach and support the children in playing co-operatively with one another.
- Make sure that if a child is feeling anxious, there is a familiar adult or friend at hand to provide reassurance.
- Ensure that the children feel able to make mistakes and to learn from them.

Finding out more
Emotional Literacy and Mental Health in Early Years by Hannah Mortimer (QEd Publications).

WORKING WITH CARERS
● Ask parents or carers about their child's past, so that you can talk to the children about their memories and about the way they felt then.

MAKING LINKS
● Contact the health visitor if you are concerned about a child's emotional development and want to suggest more support for parents/carers.

Equal opportunities

What you need to know
● The Government's 'Full Day Care Standards' publication contains guidance on the standards that settings should aim for in all aspects of childcare, including the provision of equal opportunities.
● Standard 9 states that a 'registered person' and staff should actively promote equality of opportunity and anti-discriminatory practice for all children. Often, this 'registered person' is the SENCO.
● To do this, the registered person should have, and periodically review, an equal opportunity policy that is consistent with current legislation and guidance. All children and adults should be treated with equal concern and the registered person should consider relevant anti-discriminatory good practice.
● The registered person should also promote equal opportunities with regard to employment, training, admission to day care and access to the resources, activities and facilities available.

How to help
● All staff and volunteers should understand and implement the equal opportunity policy.
● Look at ways in which you can develop your anti-discriminatory practice. Here are some ideas.

- A setting whose practice is anti-discriminatory will be one where differences in identities, cultures, religions, abilities and social practices are valued and celebrated.
- A setting whose practice is anti-discriminatory will recognise the impact of the social inequalities that exist in wider society and their effect on the lives of young children and their families.
- A setting whose practice is anti-discriminatory will value children and adults for their individuality and ensure a sense of belonging that promotes self-esteem. It will respect where children come from and what they bring to the learning situation.
- A setting whose practice is anti-discriminatory is one where the importance of what is learned and unlearned in the early years is fully appreciated.

Finding out more
Disability Equality in the Classroom: a Human Rights Issue by Richard Rieser and Micheline Mason is published by Disability Equality in Education (who also provide training): Unit GL, Leroy House, 436 Essex Road, London N1 3QP. Their resources catalogue is available from the website, www.diseed.org.uk.

WORKING WITH CARERS
● Parents and carers should have access to the equal opportunities policy.
● The registered person should liaise with parents/carers to ensure that all children's records contain information that enables the best care to be given to their child.
● Look for ways of welcoming and accepting all children and their families, breaking down family isolation and building trusting relationships.

MAKING LINKS
● Contact your local Early Years Partnership, Sure Start or Joint Training Forum, for equal opportunities training.

Family breakdown

What you need to know
● At least one in four families in the UK has one parent absent for some reason, and in 90 per cent of these families it is the father. About one child in eight is likely to experience family divorce before the age of ten, and about a third of these children are under five.
● For some children, a family breakdown may have become a fact of life. For others, it will be a new experience. Feelings may still be raw and sensitive, and you will need to plan how you are going to

support that child best through the next few months.
● Children adjust best to the change if they continue to feel loved and valued by both parents, even though they live apart. Children whose parents discuss with them what is going on appear to cope better. They need clear information in a way that they can understand.

How to help
● Try to understand what family breakdown means from the child's point of view. A family breakdown can take them utterly by surprise and cause misery and bewilderment. Coming just at a time when the parents will be absorbed in their own conflicts and emotions, this can leave the child feeling isolated, and even in some way responsible for the split.
● Make sure that your setting is an important 'constant' at a time when home life might be confusing and unsettled. Keep to your familiar routines and make allowances if the child wants to play with very familiar or less demanding activities for a while.
● Some children may be feeling very miserable or cross. Others may behave as if nothing is wrong, but may show a delayed reaction later or show you through their atypical behaviour that they are unsettled. Make allowances for difficult behaviour and stay calm and reassuring as you handle it firmly and consistently, but lovingly too.
● Concentrate on making the child feel secure and comforted during the session.

Finding out more
● Send for some 'Divorce and Separation' leaflets from the 'Understanding Childhood' series, The Child Psychotherapy Trust, Star House, 104–108 Grafton Road, London NW5 4BD, www.childpsychotherapytrust.org.uk.

WORKING WITH CARERS
● It will be helpful for you to sensitively gather the facts from the parent or carer, and establish what the child knows. Agree the factual information you may need to give the child, and decide on one carer in your setting who is going to be giving particular support.

MAKING LINKS
● Try and maintain links with both parents and share information with all those who still have 'parental responsibility'.

Family therapy

What you need to know
● You may occasionally have a child in your setting who is attending family therapy sessions with other members of their family.
● Sometimes this is related to a problem you already know about, for example a behavioural or emotional difficulty in one of the children, or a family breakdown.
● Difficult behaviours or emotional problems can have complex causes, and it sometimes makes sense for a specialist to work with the whole family. This might be to work on their expectations and relationships and to help them pull together as a family unit, yet value each other as individuals.
● At other times, you may not understand why they are attending family therapy as the reasons are confidential and do not concern the setting. For example, perhaps there was a bereavement long ago, that is affecting how the family handle day-to-day situations now.
● Most family therapy sessions are conducted by a therapist

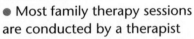

and co-therapist, often with other professionals observing and making suggestions. There are different models of therapy which different teams adopt.
● Usually the whole family is seen together, occasionally with extended family members as well.

How to help
● If a child is absent from the setting for regular family therapy sessions, try to support this by providing opportunities for the child to catch up on missed activities or just to play quietly for a while if the child seems unsettled.
● Sometimes children's behaviour may be unsettled or excitable after a session, because of sensitive matters or strong feelings that have arisen. Provide a quiet corner for the child to play through any remaining emotions or let them take a lively run outside to spend some energy.
● Occasionally a family might go through a stage of feeling angry at the therapist. This is sometimes part of the process of pulling together more and it may actually lead to positive change.

Finding out more
Read *Helping Families with Troubled Children* by Carole Sutton (Wiley).

WORKING WITH CARERS
● Reassure parents and carers that they should find the session challenging but helpful.
● Offer (through parents/carers) to work with the therapists by sending information or planning special activities for the child if this would help.

MAKING LINKS
● Family therapy services can usually be found within the NHS child and family CAMHS teams, in social services and also in certain voluntary organisations.

Hearing Impairment

What you need to know
● Many early years children suffer from temporary, fluctuating, or even permanent hearing loss.
● About 840 children a year are born with a permanent hearing impairment, and thousands more will have a temporary loss.
● Temporary hearing loss can often be a result of colds that have caused ear infections.
● Other children have a build up of mucus in the middle ear that stops the sounds being transmitted properly, leading to 'conductive deafness'. This is known as 'glue ear' and is often treated at hospital by draining the mucus and then inserting grommets.
● 'Sensori-neural deafness' usually means that sounds are not being processed correctly in the inner ear. Sometimes this can follow rubella, mumps or meningitis. This is likely to be a permanent hearing impairment.
● In 'mixed deafness', children may have a mixture of conductive and sensori-neural hearing impairment. Very few children are completely deaf.
● Some children need hearing aids to amplify the sound. Cochlear implants are a kind of hearing aid which send electrical signals to the brain. Radio aids help you communicate clearly to the child even if there is background noise.

How to help
● You are in a good position to identify hearing difficulties early on. Early identification of hearing impairment is vital because it affects language development.
● Make sure you have the child's attention before speaking.
● Ensure that you are in front of the child and at the same level.
● Keep background noise down by using soft surfaces that will absorb sound.
● Make sure that spaces are well lit so that you can see faces clearly.
● Speak clearly and slowly, and do not shout.
● Keep up to date with any signs the child might be using, so that you can use and understand these and clarify what is being said.
● Take a note of unusual words, or words the child does not understand, so that you can build the correct words into their practical experiences.

Finding out more
RNID have recently published *Effective Early Intervention for Deaf Children 0–5 and Their Families*. Contact the information line at the Royal National Institute for Deaf People, freephone: 0808 808 01 23 or visit their website at: www.rnid.org.uk.

WORKING WITH CARERS
● Speak with the parents and health visitor if you have concerns about a child's hearing.

MAKING LINKS
● Contact your local service for Hearing Impaired Children through the LEA or Early Years Partnership.

SPECIAL NEEDS **in the early years:** The essential A–Z guide to special needs

HIV/AIDS

What you need to know

● AIDS is caused by a virus called 'HIV' ('Human Immunodeficiency Virus') which can damage the body's ability to defend itself against certain infections.

● Blood tests can be used to detect whether a person is 'HIV-positive' (carrying the HIV virus). People who are HIV-positive usually go on to develop AIDS at some point, though the timescale is extremely variable and treatments are improving

● It is transmitted by an exchange of fluids, for example from an infected mother to an unborn child.

● Improved medication has helped greatly to improve the life expectancy of babies born to HIV-positive mothers. Many live to several years or more before experiencing illness.

● Young children are not likely to know that there is anything wrong unless they become ill.

● Children with HIV only pose a small risk to others, though they may themselves be prone to dangerous infections.

● There is no evidence that HIV can be transmitted by everyday social contact, cuddles, coughs, sneezes, tears, saliva or sharing a toilet seat.

How to help

● Take sensible precautions whenever dealing with bleeding incidents for *all* children. Wear protective gloves and dispose of all blood and bodily fluid products safely.

● Normal everyday standards of good hygiene are quite sufficient – follow the first aid and health and safety guidelines of your particular setting or local authority.

● Maintain confidentiality; parents/carers are under no obligation to tell you that their child has HIV. Operate a 'need to know' policy.

● Warn all parents/carers about any virulent infections going round, such as measles or chicken pox.

Finding out more

The Terence Higgins Trust: 52–54 Grays Inn Road, London WC1X 8JU. Helpline: 020 7242 1010. Website: www.tht.org.uk.

WORKING WITH CARERS

● You may not be told that a child has HIV, though many parents tell at least one member of staff so that they can be alerted about particular infections in the setting.

● Remember that parents may have their own health problems and need your extra understanding and support as well.

MAKING LINKS

● Build up a resource library for colleagues and parents, so that everyone becomes better informed about the condition. Share accurate information and try to dispel any myths and misunderstandings.

SPECIAL NEEDS in the early years

IEP

What you need to know

● Individual education plans should be a key feature of planning for any SEN in your group either as part of your Early Years Action (see page 28) or your Early Years Action Plus (see page 29).
● They should contain three or four short-term targets and make it clear how you will know that your teaching has been successful.
● They should lead to the child making progress and should be an integrated aspect of the curriculum planning for the whole group.
● They should only include that which is additional to or different from the regular early years curriculum that is in place for all the children.

How to help

● There is no set format, and you need to design an IEP that is clear, accessible and understandable for your setting.
● You might include: the name of the child; whether you are planning Early Years Action or Early Years Action Plus; the nature of the child's difficulty; a list of the child's strengths; the action you are planning; the names of those involved in the work in the setting; the help that will come from parents or carers; three or four targets for the term; your monitoring and assessment arrangements; when you will review the IEP with parents/carers and who else you will invite to the meeting.
● Targets should be 'SMART' – specific, measurable, achievable, realistic and time bound, for example: 'By the end of this term, Joe will be able to play with another child in the sand for ten minutes without fighting and when one of us is close by.'
● The IEP should underpin all your planning and intervention for the child with learning difficulties and should therefore be shared with colleagues, parents and carers.
● It must include *what* should be taught, *how* it should be taught and *how often* the additional or different provision will be made.
● Use the IEP to show how you will differentiate your activities (see page 28) in order to make the curriculum accessible to those children who have SEN.

Finding out more

You will find examples of individual education plans in other books in this series, in particular the *Special Needs Handbook* by Hannah Mortimer (Scholastic).

WORKING WITH CARERS
● IEPs need to be reviewed with parents or carers at least once a term and should clearly show the help that parents and carers have agreed to put in as well.

MAKING LINKS
● Your SENCO or Area SENCO will be able to provide you with help and support on writing IEPs and putting them into practice.

Inclusion

What you need to know
● The idea of inclusion is now firmly embedded within the SEN Code of Practice (see page 21) and the SEN Disability Act (see page 25).
● When children with SEN used to be integrated into mainstream provision, they attended their local setting *if they could cope*. Inclusion goes much further – children attend their local setting *because they are there*. Only if it is proved that their needs cannot be met there, might a more specialist placement be sought.
● Inclusion is a journey and not a destination: each LEA differs in how far their policies have come along that road.

How to help
● If you are making use of extra adult support for a child with SEN, employ careful joint-planning to make sure that the child is fully included and has the opportunity to function as independently as possible.
● Use educational labels rather than categories or medical labels (such as 'co-ordination difficulty' rather than 'dyspraxia', or even 'child who has SEN' rather than 'SEN child').
● Be good role models for the children by providing positive expectations and in the way you respect and value the children.

● Do all that you can to improve children's communication skills, for example, by teaching signing to everyone or using a communication book to show ways in which a severely disabled child makes his or her needs known.
● Use teaching strategies that enable *all* children to join in the activities and to learn from them.
● Plan individual approaches that are based on pupils' earlier experiences, which set high expectations, and which encourage the children to support each other.
● Plan all your support flexibly and creatively, so that it promotes joining in and inclusion and does not create barriers and exclusion.
● So often, an activity can be changed in some way to suit individual needs. You should never exclude certain children from an activity because they cannot 'fit in' with it.

Finding out more
The Index for Inclusion: Developing Learning and Participation in Schools is published by the CSIE (Centre for Studies on Inclusive Education), New Redland, Frenchay Campus, Coldharbour Lane, Bristol, BS16 1QU. A list of further publications is available on their website: http://inclusion.uwe.ac.uk.

WORKING WITH CARERS
● Gather as much information as you can from parents and carers about a child with disability. This will enable you to set high expectations and build on their strengths while supporting their weaknesses.

MAKING LINKS
● Many LEAs now employ early years inclusion officers – contact your local office for details.

Independence training

What you need to know
● Young children vary greatly in the ages at which they achieve personal independence in areas like getting dressed by themselves, using the toilet or feeding themselves.
● Some strive for independence, even if it is obvious at times that they still need help. Others are quite content to have everything done for them.

● Children who have SEN may have more difficulties than others in acquiring independence skills, perhaps because their hands are still clumsy, they have short attention spans, or they are not able to plan ahead so well.

How to help
● Learn to provide just the right amount of help, and no more for a child to whom you are teaching independence skills.
● Allow plenty of time for a child to dress or undress independently. Stay close to encourage and celebrate their successes.
● Think ahead about the independence skills necessary for school and break these down into easy steps that you can teach the child.
● Teach step-by-step and then link the steps together so that the child is managing more complex tasks.
● Offer reasons and explanations for rules at a level the child can understand, giving clear examples. Try to offer choices wherever possible, and set up situations so that the child can exercise their ability to be as independent as possible in the setting.
● Toilets need to be accessible and welcoming, washbasins reachable, coat pegs low and dressing-up clothes easy to put on. Craft materials should be easy to reach, water and drinks in jugs small enough to pour from, and choices given for activities wherever it is possible.

Finding out more
Portage is a home-based step-by-step approach for helping parents/carers teach their disabled children to develop. You will find the address of the national association in 'Useful contacts' on page 63. The Portage training courses offer many ideas for developing independence skills.

WORKING WITH CARERS
● Encourage parents or carers to become familiar with how much their child can do without help, and just how much help is required. They should then help the child with those parts of any routine task that need it, but also stand back at the right moment for their child to complete the task by themselves.

MAKING LINKS
● If a child's self-help skills are affected by their disability, the paediatric occupational therapist might be able to advise you.

Learning difficulties

What you need to know
● These are the legal definitions given in the 1996 Education Act (Section 312) that it would be useful for you to know.

> Children are described as having 'special educational needs' if they have a 'learning difficulty' which needs 'special educational provision' to be made for them.
> Children have a learning difficulty if they have a difficulty in learning that is significantly different from the majority of children of the same age, or have a disability which prevents or hinders them from making use of educational facilities of a kind usually provided for children of the same age in schools within the area of the local education authority.
> Children are also said to have a learning difficulty if they are under five and fall within the definitions above *or would do if special educational provision were not made for them.*

● In practice, 'special educational provision' means that you are having to provide support that is *additional or different* to usual. Given that your setting already has to be flexible enough to meet the needs of a wide range of developmental stages and individuals, it should be possible to meet the needs of most early years children inclusively in their local settings.

How to help
● Sometimes the reason for a child's learning difficulty is known – perhaps there is a diagnosis or a recognised disability. In other cases, it appears that the child is simply developing more slowly. You do not always need to know the reason to be able to support the child.
● Instead, use your methods of observation and assessment to work out the child's strengths and weaknesses and take Early Years Action (see page 28) to address their needs.
● Use differentiation (see page 28) to make your activities more accessible to the child so that they can take as full a part as possible in your Foundation Stage curriculum.

Finding out more
MENCAP, www.mencap.org.uk is a support organisation for children with severe learning difficulties and their families.

WORKING WITH CARERS
● Coming to terms with the fact that their child has learning difficulties can be a distressing time for parents and carers. Try to tune into the feelings of disbelief, anger, sorrow, guilt or protectiveness that they might be feeling.

MAKING LINKS
● If you feel that you need more specialist assessment and advice, then discuss this with the SENCO and consider planning Early Years Action Plus (see page 29).

Medical difficulties

What you need to know

● About ten to 15 per cent of children under sixteen are affected by chronic, long-term physical or medical problems.

● The most common conditions are eczema (eight to ten per cent of children), asthma (two to five per cent), diabetes (1.8 per cent), congenital heart disease (about 0.5 per cent) and epilepsy (also around 0.5 per cent).

● There are many other potentially frightening or painful conditions that are less common and many of these have an unpredictable course. These conditions include: sickle cell anaemia; rheumatoid arthritis; HIV infections and AIDS; cystic fibrosis; cancer and leukaemia.

● The DfES and Department of Health have published a pack *Supporting Pupils with Medical Needs: A Good Practice Guide* which helps you draw up a policy.

How to help

● Collect all the information you require from parents, carers and health professionals. You need to understand what the medical condition means for the child, what it means for you, what to look out for and what you should know.

● When talking about a child's medical condition, concentrate on the here and now.

● Help the child find words for how they are feeling, what is happening and what will happen next.

● Impending visits to hospital and clinics can be frightening until a child understands exactly what will happen. Talk with parents or carers if this is the case and use your regular play activities to help.

● Young children make sense of their world by mastering the familiar routines and rules that form their day. You can help in the setting by keeping routines as familiar as possible when a child has a chronic condition or illness.

● You can also make links between the home and group, or with the hospital or hospice, so that you keep familiar activities and contacts going during a period of absence.

Finding out more

There is more information in *Medical Difficulties* by Hannah Mortimer from this series, *Special Needs in the Early Years* (Scholastic). The DfES publication *Supporting Pupils with Medical Needs* is available from www.teachernet.gov.uk.

WORKING WITH CARERS

● Talk with parents if medication is needed in the setting. There is no legal duty that requires you to administer medication – this is a voluntary role. However, it can make all the difference between whether or not a child can attend your early years setting.

● Make sure you have procedures in place for keeping medicines safe, recording information about dosage and signing when it has been administered. You will find full guidance in the DfES publication mentioned above.

MAKING LINKS

● The local school nurse or health visitor might be able to provide staff with information and training on a particular medical condition.

Meningitis

What you need to know

● 'Meningitis' literally means 'inflammation of the meninges', which is the membrane lining the brain and the spinal cord.

● It can be caused by different kinds of germs, and how serious it is depends on the germ involved. The early symptoms usually look the same to a layperson.

● Bacterial meningitis is quite rare, with around 2000 reported cases per year in the UK. However, it can be very serious and needs urgent treatment with antibiotics.

● Viral meningitis is more common and is rarely life-threatening although it can make the sufferer feel very weak and poorly. Antibiotics are not effective with viral meningitis, so this is usually treated with nursing, rest and care.

● The germs can be spread by coughing, sneezing and very close contact, but do not survive for long outside the body. They are not likely to be passed through toys and equipment, though good hygiene practice should obviously always be followed.

● The symptoms can look very like flu to begin with – a fever, vomiting, headache, and a marked stiffness, particularly at the back of the neck.

● The child turns away from any bright light, might complain of joint stiffness, and, in time, becomes drowsy and dull. Sometimes the child develops fits and a widespread blotchy rash or bruising associated with blood poisoning or septicaemia.

● The illness sometimes develops over one or two days, but can come on very quickly in a matter of a few hours. In these cases, it becomes clear very soon that the child is very ill indeed and emergency treatment should be sought.

How to help

● Make sure you and your colleagues are aware of the symptoms of meningitis and take immediate action if you suspect that a child might be affected.

● Contact parents or carers and suggest an immediate visit to the GP or the accident and emergency department.

● If the child is difficult to rouse, call an ambulance.

● Children who are recovering from viral meningitis can feel weak, debilitated and depressed for some time afterwards. These children may feel floppy, tired and irritable and might need your patience and reassurance for several weeks.

● You might find that new skills learned in pre-school have been lost and need to be retaught.

Finding out more

Local health clinics carry information pamphlets, or contact the Meningitis Research Foundation (www.meningitis.org).

WORKING WITH CARERS

● Keep a particular note of the child's hearing since this may well have been affected and the parents may need to request an up-to-date check.

MAKING LINKS

● If a child has been hospitalised for some time, make contact with the hospital teacher to see whether it would be appropriate to send in some suitable activities.

Multiple difficulties

What you need to know
● Some children are profoundly disabled in all areas of their development and learning. They may have been described as having 'profound and multiple learning difficulties'.

● There are many different reasons for children experiencing multiple difficulties. Sometimes, difficulties have arisen because of brain injury around birth or some other trauma. Perhaps something went wrong with their development very early in pregnancy, affecting the way in which their bodies and brains developed, or there is a chromosomal abnormality or other syndrome associated with profound developmental delay.

● There can be enormous benefits from meeting their needs in an inclusive early years setting, so long as needs have been carefully assessed, everybody works as a team, and the children can be supported appropriately.

● Usually, these children will have a 'statement of special educational needs' from the local education authority, describing their needs and the resources needed to meet those needs.

How to help
● The child is likely to have a special support assistant allocated for their care. Try not to regard this person as 'the expert', but share care and encouragement with all colleagues so that you all develop skills in meeting the child's needs.

● Talk to parents or carers about how the child makes their needs known. Put together a communication book with photographs of the child and what their various expressions and behaviours mean. This can then be shared with all colleagues.

● You may need a quiet corner for some peace and soft music if the child indicates that he or she is sleepy.

● Look for activities where the child can feel and touch things and can enjoy interacting with others, at whatever level.

● Talk to the child constantly, looking for ways of helping him or her to link 'cause' with 'effect', an important stage in early development. Try playing 'Peek-a-boo' games.

Finding out more
Assessing Communication in the Classroom by Clare Latham and Ann Miles (David Fulton Publishers).

WORKING WITH CARERS
● Make a special welcome to the parents and carers, who might have had a difficult time coming to terms with their child's condition. It will be an anxious period while they see how their child is coping in your setting, and whether you are meeting their child's needs.

MAKING LINKS
● Find out which other professionals are involved so that you can share approaches and seek advice on 'next steps'. There is probably a local child development centre team involved (see page 19).

Parent supporters

What you need to know

- Most LEAs appoint 'parent partnership officers' to offer advice and to support parents/carers at any stage of the assessment process.
- They work alongside educational psychologists, support teachers, education social workers and office support staff, but are also able to give independent advice. They can listen to carers' worries and concerns and explain the statutory assessment processes to them.
- There are also 'independent parental supporters' who can help parents and carers through their child's statutory assessment (see page 58) and will stay in contact afterwards.
- When the LEA issues a child's statement, they must give the parents/carers details of somebody who can give support, advice and information as well as telling them the 'named officer' of the LEA from whom further information can be obtained.

How to help

- If a parent would like an independent parental supporter while their child is being statutorily assessed, help them to contact the Parent Partnership Officer at the Education Department so they can discuss this.
- It may also be possible for them to be introduced to an independent parental supporter through a support group or through a local volunteer centre. Find out about local voluntary organisations in your area through the local Council for Voluntary Services, or through the NCVO directory (see below).
- Explain to parents or carers that many of these independent parental supporters are themselves carers for children with special needs who have volunteered to support other families.
- Never underestimate the support that you yourself can offer to the parents or carers of a child who has SEN. You do not need to know all the answers – simply where to find them out.
- Parents in similar situations can offer invaluable support to each other. Seek mutual permission before passing on names. You might offer your setting as a place for a support group to meet.

Finding out more

The *Contact a Family Directory* can be obtained on subscription from Contact a Family, Equity House, 209–211 City Road, London, EC1V 1JN. It lists the various support organisations associated with different conditions. The 'Contact a Family' website (www.cafamily.org.uk) may also be useful. The National Council for Voluntary Organisations publishes a list of voluntary service providers throughout the country. Visit their website, www.ncvo-vol.org.uk.

WORKING WITH CARERS

- Parent partnership officers can help parents to say what they think their child's needs are and help the child's views to be represented. If there are difficulties or misunderstandings between parents and LEAs, then the parent partnership officer will try to resolve them.

MAKING LINKS

- Visits to prospective schools and support sessions might also be arranged as part of the parent partnership officer's service.

SPECIAL NEEDS in the early years

Physical difficulties

What you need to know

● Children who have physical and co-ordination difficulties have a wide range of needs. Some might have mobility difficulties and are not yet walking. Others may have fine-motor problems and find it hard to dress, hold a pencil or make small finger movements.

● Sometimes this will be because of a recognised condition, such as cerebral palsy (see page 18) or spina bifida (see page 56).

● Sometimes their physical development is delayed for their age because of other developmental difficulties.

● Sometimes they are 'clumsy' and their co-ordination is still immature, perhaps because they have a learning difficulty such as dyspraxia (see page 27).

● Children with mobility difficulties have the same needs as all children – to play, make friends and access the Foundation Stage curriculum.

● Some children will have been given special equipment to help them sit, stand, move and balance.

How to help

● Try to see your setting from the point of view of the child with mobility difficulties. Are your floor surfaces clean and welcoming? Are they comfortable to crawl or roll on? Are there areas for running toys and wheeled toys and have you provided other areas safe for floor play?

● Are your toys and equipment accessible for a child with mobility difficulties? Can the child still make choices and play independently? Are your spaces accessible to children in wheelchairs or with rollators? Can they open doors, reach for equipment and play at the same physical level as the other children?

● Know when to 'stand back' and allow the child to be independent.

● Provide opportunities for playing together in different positions: lying; kneeling; sitting or standing at a table.

● Ensure that your picture books and stories reflect a wide range of ability, including children who use wheelchairs.

Finding out more

Physical and Co-ordination Difficulties by Hannah Mortimer from this series, *Special Needs in the Early Years* (Scholastic).

WORKING WITH CARERS
● Consider parents as the 'experts' on their child's physical condition. Parents can also show you how to use any special equipment.

MAKING LINKS
● Contact the physiotherapist or occupational therapist for advice on equipment, seating and positioning.

SPECIAL NEEDS **in the early years:** The essential A–Z guide to special needs

Play therapy

What you need to know

● Young children cannot always tell you what is wrong – sometimes they simply do not know and sometimes they lack the words to describe how they feel.

● It is often possible to observe them express their feelings through their play. For example, we can observe an older brother or sister playing with the dolls, acting out considerable feelings of love, anger or fantasy after the arrival of a new baby in the family.

● Sometimes it is feasible to observe the way children play and interpret how they are thinking about their life and what has happened to them. This is very helpful for children who are emotionally vulnerable or who have been negatively affected by events in their lives.

● Over the years, psychologists have developed ways of interpreting children's play and the readiness with which they absorb themselves in 'miniature worlds'.

● This has led to complex methods of interpreting a child's play and also helping them to make sense of their feelings through a method known as 'play therapy'.

How to help

● These approaches have evolved following careful research and understanding of how young children behave and develop, so they should not be used to interpret children's play too loosely. However, you can make good use of the principles in order to help all your children cope with difficult times.

- Provide a 'hospital' corner to help children play through any feelings they have about doctors and hospitals.
- Collect children's picture books about issues such as a new baby, a new family, going to the dentist and going on holiday.
- Some local library services or toy libraries lend out themed book or play packs around these kinds of subjects.
- If a child's play suddenly becomes especially violent or unusual in some way, play alongside them and give the child the opportunity to share their game with you. This might help you understand what has affected them.

Finding out more

The Magination Press specialises in books that help young children deal with personal or psychological concerns (see 'Useful contacts' on page 63 for details).

WORKING WITH CARERS

● Contact parents or carers if the child's play suddenly changes – they may be able to tell you what is happening that might have caused this. Remember the child protection procedures if you have serious concerns about the child's safety (see page 20).

MAKING LINKS

● Play therapists are psychologists or therapists usually based in NHS child and family centres. Contact your local CAMHS service or the health visitor for information.

Self-esteem

What you need to know

● It is possible to tell if a child has low self-esteem. Quite often you will notice certain characteristics and patterns of behaviour, though they are not a fixed rule.

● Of course, we all feel 'up' and 'down' on particular days depending on recent events, our general sense of well-being, our health and our moods. Children, too, have their 'good days' and their 'bad days'.

● Children who have low self-esteem often have a strong need for reassurance and often appear to be insecure and 'clingy'.

● Children with low self-esteem have a low opinion of themselves, little faith in their own capabilities and easily become tearful if things go wrong.

● Children with low self-esteem are reluctant to express their opinions and find it hard to make decisions.

● Sometimes they over-react to failure and find it hard to accept correction.

● They may seem to feel safer if they 'take control' and you might find that they are frequently 'testing boundaries' or dominating other children's play. They might tend to hurt or bully others.

How to help

● Use a warm, positive approach with each child and invest individual time in your relationship. A key-worker system in which each adult is responsible for befriending and supporting certain children can be helpful.

● Positive approaches to managing difficult behaviour help to ensure that the child's self-esteem remains intact.

● Children, who are 'nagged' constantly with 'don't…' and 'no', tend to stop listening or trying after a while and come to see themselves as 'naughty'. Children whose appropriate behaviour is noticed and admired, are more likely to repeat the behaviours that are attracting your praise and to see themselves as helpful and kind.

● Confidence and learning seem to be bound together. If a child tries something new and fails, their self-esteem and self-confidence becomes lower and they are less likely to try again.

Finding out more

The Emotional Literacy Handbook - Promoting Whole School Strategies by James Park, Alice Haddon and Harriet Goodman (David Fulton Publishers).

WORKING WITH CARERS

● Children who have warm, affectionate relationships with their parents or carers generally develop high self-esteem and a positive image of themselves. Help parents tune into their child, so that they are more able to enjoy each other's company.

MAKING LINKS

● Contact your local training forum for training on circle-time approaches – these are a helpful way to boost self-esteem.

Semantic pragmatic difficulties

What you need to know

● Some children develop speech and language reasonably well, but have subtle difficulties in understanding the social nature of language and conversation.

● Children with 'semantic and pragmatic' language difficulties have difficulties both in the understanding of abstract language and in the social use of language.

● They might stick to topics of intense interest, never wait for gaps in a conversation before cutting in, use poor eye contact, and become quickly distressed in social situations.

● They tend to take a long time to settle in an early years setting unless the adults and surroundings are very familiar.

● Usually, their understanding of abstract words is very poor (for example, quiet, kind, heavy), though their understanding of concrete and literal words can be excellent.

● Imaginative play is often missing or very limited.

● They may find it hard to see another person's point of view.

● These difficulties are rather similar to those on the autistic continuum but often improve once language skills develop.

How to help

● Sometimes these children need plenty of opportunities to hear language, listen to you talking through picture books, and feel excited enough by their play to want to talk about it. Keep the language simple.

● You will find you need to give more attention than usual, playing and talking alongside the child, and developing early conversations much as you would for a younger child, but with topics of interest appropriate to their age.

● Help these children see the other child's point of view and maintain a flow to their interaction.

● Use a light touch and make sure you are at their level in order to encourage the briefest of eye contacts as you talk to the child.

● Use a simple picture timetable to let the child know what will happen next during your session.

● Always *show* these children what to do as well as telling them.

● Help parents and carers to keep their instructions and commentary very simple, starting with key words and actions.

Finding out more

The Association for All Speech Impaired Children (AFASIC), 347 Central Markets, London EC1A 9NH. Website: www.afasic.org.uk.

WORKING WITH CARERS

● Help parents and carers keep their instructions and commentary very simple, starting with key words and actions.

MAKING LINKS

● Contact any speech and language therapist who might be involved, so that you can link in with their approaches. Parents/carers might be able to help you keep in touch through a regular notebook.

SEN

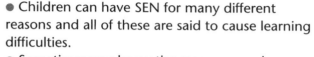

What you need to know

● You may find that there are some children in your group who seem to need *additional* or *different* approaches to help them play and develop, even after they have had time to settle with you and you have tried all your usual approaches.

● These are the children who are said to have special educational needs (SEN).

● Children can have SEN for many different reasons and all of these are said to cause learning difficulties.

● Sometimes you know the reasons – perhaps a child has a condition that affects their development, such as cerebral palsy (see page 18), or perhaps they are delayed in their ability to speak and communicate because of autism (see page 14).

● These children do not have special needs because they look different, because they have a particular label or because they behave in an unusual way. They have special needs because they fail to make acceptable progress even when you have tried all your usual approaches.

● The SEN Code of Practice gives you guidance on how to meet SEN in your setting (see page 21).

How to help

● Allow all children time to settle in and to respond to your usual approaches for differentiating the early years curriculum before you assume they have SEN.

● Start by gathering information through observation and record-keeping. You will be doing this for all the children, so your system for monitoring a child who has SEN can arise naturally from your existing approaches, but be in much more detail.

● Use diary records, photographs and examples of the child's work to build up a dossier of the child's interests, strengths, progress and areas of need.

● Checklists and observation schedules can sometimes be useful to aid what you are doing, and some groups have found it helpful to break the Stepping Stones down into even smaller stages for recording progress.

Finding out more

For more information, read *The SEN Code of Practice in Early Years Settings* by Hannah Mortimer (QEd Publications) available from www.qed.uk.com. *Removing Barriers to Achievement: The Government's Strategy for SEN* is available from the DfES and can be accessed at www.teachernet.gov.uk/wholeschool/sen/senstrategy.

WORKING WITH CARERS
● Look for methods of assessment and observation that include what is happening at home and that involve families.

MAKING LINKS
● Sometimes children will join your group with a disability or special need already identified. If so, there should be information available to you from parents and other professionals.

SENCO

What you need to know

● The importance of having a 'special educational needs co-ordinator' ('SENCO') in every early years setting has been stated clearly in government guidance.

● While the setting's headteacher or manager and the SENCO are there to advise and support colleagues, provision for children with special educational needs is the responsibility of everyone in the setting, and everyone should be aware of your policy.

● In practice, the division of day-to-day responsibilities for meeting SEN is a matter for individual settings.

● The SENCO works with managers, governors and senior staff to put together, monitor and review the SEN policy for the setting (see page 52).

● The main responsibility of a setting-based SENCO is to work with all staff to make sure that the SEN policy works effectively and inclusively, and to provide information to other members of staff.

How to help

● Find out from the SENCO what the procedures are in your setting for working with and including disabled children and those with other forms of SEN.

● Ask the SENCO for advice about how to identify, support and monitor these children's needs – if the SENCO does not know, then they should find out for you.

● If you feel that a child might have SEN, discuss this with the SENCO and decide whether that child's name should be added to your SEN register or equivalent recording system.

● Talk to the SENCO if you feel you need more information on any child with SEN. There is likely to be a confidential file with information and correspondence on children with SEN and it might be appropriate for you to have access to this.

● The SENCO should be able to support you in making observations and in setting appropriate targets for meeting individual children's needs and entitlements through an IEP (see page 38).

Finding out more

The *SENCO Handbook – Supporting Colleagues in Early Years Settings* by Hannah Mortimer from this series, *Special Needs in the Early Years* (Scholastic).

WORKING WITH CARERS

● Although it may not be the SENCO's direct responsibility to liaise with every individual parent or carer of a child with SEN, the SENCO must support staff to make sure communication takes place smoothly and effectively.

● The SENCO should also be responsible for supporting staff in meetings or reviews with parents, and in setting appropriate targets, review dates and times.

MAKING LINKS

● The SENCO can keep you in touch with any national or local developments on provision for children with SEN, arrange training for you and make links with outside agencies.

SEN policy

What you need to know
● Each setting should have a policy for SEN, which is monitored and revised regularly.
● It is the SENCO's responsibility to work with the team to produce a written SEN policy and make sure it is cross-referenced to other relevant policies, such as the admissions policy and the equal opportunities policy.
● The policy should begin with a short summary of the beliefs shared by staff regarding pupils with SEN.
● The policy should then show how staff:

- ensure the entitlement for all children to the curriculum
- monitor, record and evaluate all children's progress
- identify, assess and review SEN
- provide additional resources and support for children with SEN.

● The policy should also indicate how staff work with parents, carers and agencies, and detail the training and expertise already existing.

How to help
● Make sure that you have read and are familiar with your setting's SEN policy.
● Remember that it is each staff member's responsibility to implement the policy, so speak to the SENCO if you are not sure what you should be doing.
● You should have an IEP in place for each child with SEN (see page 38) and you should be clear on how you are going to put this into practice and what progress you are looking for in the child.
● Think about how effective the policy is for the children you work with and for your own practice. Take an active part in feeding this back to the SENCO ready for the regular policy review.
● Inform the SENCO of any training or particular experience you have had in SEN so that this can appear in the policy.
● You should find recent and relevant information in the SEN policy about the support services available to you and how these are accessed in your setting. Help to keep information up to date in the light of your experience.

Finding out more
All Together – How to Provide Inclusive Services for Young Disabled Children and Their Families by Mary Dickins with Judy Denziloe (National Children's Bureau). *Removing Barriers to Achievement: The Government's Strategy for SEN* is available from the DfES and can be accessed at www.teachernet.gov.uk/wholeschool/sen/senstrategy.

WORKING WITH CARERS
● The SEN policy should show how staff share the responsibility for meeting SEN with parents, how they share information and how they respond to parental concerns.

MAKING LINKS
● The SEN policy should also show how staff work with LEAs, health services, social services and other agencies on any matter to do with the setting's SEN work.

Separation anxiety

What you need to know

● It is absolutely normal for a young child to be anxious and mildly distressed when they first separate from a parent or carer and come into your setting.

● This is part of the normal pattern of attachment (see page 12). The distress usually passes quickly as the child settles in, is reassured by other friendly and welcoming adults and as they realise that their carer will always return for them.

● Each child is individual in this respect – some children (often those with older siblings) separate and settle from the very first day, without any problems.

● A few children continue to be distressed after the first fortnight and cannot be consoled or become 'frozen' and isolated in the setting. These children are sometimes said to have 'separation anxiety'.

● Separation anxiety can also develop suddenly – after a family breakdown, bereavement or other major event.

How to help

● Plan visits for new starters and their parents and carers, gradually extending their time with you. If possible, arrange home visits too so that children can begin to form an attachment with you before they join the setting.

● Arrange for a key worker to greet and distract the child, calmly but confidently. Aim to help the child develop an attachment to a familiar adult in the setting as a 'next step' for them.

● Remember that parents and carers too will have their separation anxiety. Suggest that they peep through the window to see just how quickly their child has settled – but to take care not to be spotted!

● Use a cuddly toy as a security object in the setting. In time, the child may be happy to place it on a special shelf to 'watch'.

● Plan 'transfer objects' when a child first arrives – something the child has brought from home to show you perhaps. This eases the transfer from home to setting. Allow the child to arrive a little early or a little late if this helps.

● It is fine to allow a parent or carer to come in with a highly anxious child for a while, but make this part of a planned progression aimed towards helping the child become more emotionally independent.

Finding out more

Behavioural and Emotional Difficulties by Hannah Mortimer from this series, *Special Needs in the Early Years* (Scholastic).

WORKING WITH CARERS

● If a child suddenly becomes highly anxious on separation, talk with parents and carers and see what might be worrying them.

MAKING LINKS

● Talk with the health visitor if you are still concerned.

Specific learning difficulties (including dyslexia)

What you need to know

● Some children seem to have a specific difficulty in reading, writing, or calculating, despite being of average intelligence and managing other aspects of their learning well. These children are sometimes said to have a 'specific learning difficulty'.

● It is called 'specific' because the difficulty is greater than you might expect, given the child's obvious intelligence and ability. Dyslexia is the most familiar.

● Some teachers use the words 'specific learning difficulty' and 'dyslexia' to mean the same thing. It is important to know that there are many types of specific learning difficulty all related, although individual to the child concerned.

● In order to plan the best ways of helping, you need to know what the specific learning difficulty actually means to the child – perhaps they have a weak memory for what they see or hear, or perhaps they cannot distinguish the sounds within words.

● Since the word 'dyslexia' literally means 'cannot read', you would not expect to be identifying this in the early years.

● However, some researchers have found that certain signs of dyslexia can be recognised even in the early years before reading and writing have been taught, such as a difficulty in hearing rhyming words or a slight clumsiness when balancing.

How to help

● Do not worry if young children 'mirror write' – this is common up to the age of six, especially in children with mixed-handedness.

● Work on developing the child's general language skills and improving their vocabulary.

● Enjoy nursery rhymes together and play rhyming games.

● Practise sequencing tasks, for example arranging pictures of a simple story in order.

● Use a phonic approach (learning letter sounds) at an early age.

● Use game-like approaches to inspire motivation and confidence when introducing early literacy and numeracy skills.

● Use multi-sensory approaches to learning in which the child sees, hears, feels and manipulates.

● Teach looking and listening skills.

● Use music and songs to teach sequences, such as counting, days of the week or the alphabet.

Finding out more

Working with Children with Specific Learning Difficulties in the Early Years by Dorothy Smith (QEd Publications), available from www.qed.uk.com.

WORKING WITH CARERS

● Specific learning difficulties often run in families and taking a relevant family history can help you identify if a child might be at risk.

MAKING LINKS

● Contact the early years support teacher or the learning support services for advice and information.

Speech and language difficulties

What you need to know
- Some children's speech and language development is delayed, but is nevertheless progressing along normal lines. Perhaps these children are delayed in other areas of their development as well and language is just one part of this immaturity.
- Some children lack the ability to make certain sounds or cannot co-ordinate the sounds in the required sequence. These children are sometimes described as having 'dyspraxic', 'dysarthric' or 'articulation' difficulties.
- Some children cannot speak clearly or their language remains rather fragmented.
- For others, there is a specific language disorder which means that they would benefit from specialist therapy and approaches.
- For these children, their *understanding* of language (their *receptive* language) is usually affected as well as their *use* of language (their *expressive* language).

How to help
- Start by assessing the child's speech and language by observing their interactions and by recording extracts.
- Always make sure you have assessed how a child makes their needs known so that you can respond appropriately. This might involve you making a personal communication book for each child with SEN, or learning to use signs.
- Make sure that each child's hearing has been checked.
- If you are concerned that a child does not understand you, try giving simple instructions out of context, for example: 'Please get your coat', when it is not home time. This will help you assess whether the child can understand your words.
- Plan plenty of opportunities for developing concepts – Demonstrate examples of concepts, such as 'empty', 'lots', 'long', so that the child can make links in thinking and learn to generalise the word to new situations.
- *Time* can be a particularly hard concept for a child with receptive language difficulties. Use visual timetables and fixed, absolute examples ('*When* you have had your drink, *then* you play outside').
- Keep your language simple and clear, emphasising key words and showing children what to do as well as telling them.
- Try not to overload children with language as they can become frustrated quickly and may 'switch off' from what you are saying.

Finding out more
Speech and Language Difficulties by Hannah Mortimer from this series, *Special Needs in the Early Years* (Scholastic) or contact AFASIC, www.afasic.org.uk.

WORKING WITH CARERS
- Ask parents or carers to keep a home-setting-therapy diary, so that you can follow through any speech and language therapy advice with the child.

MAKING LINKS
- Speech and language therapists provide specialist assessment of all aspects of children's speech, language and communication and can work with families and settings on the best ways to help.
- Contact the parents or health visitor if you feel a referral might be necessary.

SPECIAL NEEDS in the early years

Spina bifida and hydrocephalus

What you need to know
● The condition of spina bifida is present from birth and affects the child's physical and neurological development.
● Spina bifida is a fault in the spinal column in which one of the vertebrae (bones that form the backbone) fails to form properly. This

leaves a gap or split. It happens very early in pregnancy and the spinal cord may not develop properly, forming a cyst or protrusion outside the spine.
● The amount of disability depends on to what extent the spinal cord is affected, where the bifida is, and the amount of nerve damage involved.
● Often, there is paralysis below the fault, with incontinence and a difficulty in or lack of walking.

How to help
● Talk to parents/carers about what the condition means for their particular child. How much aid is needed to help the child move around, reach, join in and stay clean and dry?
● If there is a buggy, special seating or standing frames, ask parents/carers for a demonstration so that you can make any adjustments necessary during the session.
● Take pains to find out about a child's strengths and interests, so that you can allow them to play independently whenever possible, rather than shadowing the child with your care and concern. Children are soon able to let you know when they need your help if you are always available and responsive.
● Any toys that encourage looking, listening, careful handling, language and imagination will be excellent – in other words, a good range of those early learning toys and activities suitable for any of your children.
● Make sure your tables and easels are at the right height for any special seats or buggies, and try to store your craft activities and toys at a level that allows all your children to make choices and reach for what they want.

Finding out more
The Association for Spina Bifida and Hydrocephalus at: ASBAH House, 42 Park Road, Peterborough PE1 2UQ. (Tel: 01733 555988, website: www.asbah.org.)

WORKING WITH CARERS
● Ask parents to show you any changing routines for the first session or two, so that you quickly become confident in taking over from them. This will be reassuring for both the parents and for you. Check with them if there is anything you need to know about the risk of infection.

MAKING LINKS
● If you find that the child is missing out on an activity because of being in the wrong position, try to contact the occupational therapist for good ideas.

Stammering

What you need to know

● Most young children pass through a stage when they begin to stammer. They find themselves full of exciting ideas, but do not have the language to express them to you. When their brain thinks faster than the words can be said, children may begin to stammer and stutter. This is absolutely normal.

● Some children seem to get stuck in this phase. They frequently stammer on words and particularly on *parts* of words. For many of these children, this seems to get worse for them at times when they feel rushed or anxious. For other children there is no pattern at all.

● Researchers feel there may be several different causes to stammering and it is not caused by anxiety alone. Most children who stammer get over their difficulties, and just a few do not.

How to help

● Never hurry the children's speech. If they are keen to tell you something, listen patiently to what they are saying, and try very hard not to interrupt or complete their thoughts for them.

● Keep looking at the child as you listen, and reply slowly and unhurriedly after a second or two's pause. This slows the whole exchange down to a more relaxed tempo.

● Try to spend more time than usual talking with that child in a relaxed situation. Children who stammer find it easiest to talk about things of personal interest to them, and most difficult when you expect them to answer questions in front of everybody.

● If it causes difficulties, do not insist on a spoken answer when you are taking the register. Ask the child to nod or give a 'thumbs-up' signal instead.

● If the child has his or her hand up in group time, let them answer fairly soon to prevent any anxiety building up.

● If words are mispronounced, do not insist on their correct pronunciation. Just repeat back the sentence slowly and correctly. Many children get syllables the wrong way round and produce the occasional spoonerism (such as 'guenpin' for 'penguin').

Finding out more

The British Stammering Association is based at: 15 Old Ford Road, London E2 9PJ. (Website: www.stammering.org.)

WORKING WITH CARERS

● Encourage parents and carers to make talking and conversation as fun as they can, so that their child joins in fully despite any difficulties. This way you can all prevent a child becoming self-conscious about a stammer.

MAKING LINKS

● Your local NHS speech and language therapy services are involved in helping families identify children who stammer and can provide specialist help and advice.

Statement of SEN

What you need to know
● For a very few children (about two per cent), the help provided by Early Years Action Plus (see page 29) will still not be sufficient to ensure satisfactory progress.
● The provider, external professionals and parents/carers may then decide to ask the LEA to consider carrying out a statutory assessment of the child's SEN.
● The LEA must decide quickly whether or not it has the evidence to indicate that a statutory assessment is necessary for a child. It is then responsible for co-ordinating the assessment and will call for the various reports that it requires, from an early years teacher, an educational psychologist, a doctor, and the social services department if involved. It will also ask parents or carers to submit their own views.
● The whole procedure must not take longer than six months unless there are exceptional circumstances.
● The statutory assessment may or may not lead to a statement of special educational needs. This states what the child's special needs are, what provision will be made for them, how the needs will be monitored, and where the child will be placed.
● It is the responsibility of the LEA to name the setting that the child should attend, taking parents' or carers' views into account.
● If a setting is the provider named on the statement, the LEA will ask the SENCO to call regular (usually six-monthly) reviews to monitor whether the child's needs are being met.

How to help
● During a statutory assessment, parents/carers will receive a number of formal letters from the LEA. The LEA is required by law to send these, and it is often helpful if staff can reassure parents and carers about their contents and put them in touch with the independent parental supporter or parent partnership officer (see page 45) if they need explanations or have concerns or queries.
● If you are approached for a report, you will be given a strict time for returning it to the LEA
● Keep all copies of IEPs and review meetings – you may need these to attach as evidence to any request for a statutory assessment.

Finding out more
Read the free leaflet 'Assessments and Statements' from the CSIE (Centre for Studies in Inclusive Education) available from New Redland, Frenchay Campus, Coldharbour Lane, Bristol, BS16 1QU. A list of further publications is available on their website: http://inclusion.uwe.ac.uk.

WORKING WITH CARERS
● Parents have various rights of appeal to an SEN tribunal if they are not happy with the statutory assessment procedures or the statement, and these are fully covered in the SEN Code of Practice.

MAKING LINKS
● Talk to your local support teacher or educational psychologist for information and advice.

Tantrums

What you need to know
● Children throw temper tantrums for a variety of reasons and you need to know why they are happening before you can decide how best to handle them.
● Some children become 'stuck' in a tantrum phase because they have learned that tantrums can achieve a desired effect.

● In general, children elicit in *you* the feelings that *they* have inside – if you are left feeling confused and muddled by a child's behaviour, it is likely that the child is feeling confused and muddled. If you are left feeling angry at the child, then it is likely that the child is feeling angry too.

How to help
● Spend time recognising and talking to the children about feelings.
● Look for ways of allowing children to get rid of pent up anger or energy by running around in a playground or beating a cushion.
● Try to work out what is causing the tantrums. Keep a diary of the big tantrums, making a note of what led up to them, what the child did, where they happened, what you did and what happened as a result of this. Then try to work out a pattern.
● Use your fairness and consistency to show the child that when you say something, you really mean it.
● Instead of saying, 'No' and, 'Don't...', give the children ideas about what they can do instead.
● When you make a request, *help* children to do as you are asking rather than doggedly insisting that they must do it themselves.
● If a child is in the full throes of a tantrum, then shouting or even reasoning will only keep the tantrum raging. Instead, the child needs a chance to calm down first (and so do you). So deal with the tantrum calmly, with minimum eye contact and words, calmly removing the child from the audience and staying close until everything 'cools down'.
● Once the child is calm again, offer comfort, talk calmly about what happened and what can be done about it.

Finding out more
There are more ideas in the book *Managing Children's Behaviour* by Hannah Mortimer from the *Early Years Training and Management* series (Scholastic).

WORKING WITH CARERS
● Explain to parents or carers that some children are very frightened by the intensity of their own tantrums and need reassurance rather than correction.

MAKING LINKS
● Contact the health visitor if you feel that a hearing or language difficulty might be contributing to the tantrums.

Toilet training

What you need to know
● There is a very wide range of ages at which children become toilet trained with confidence. Children aged between one and nearly three are all within what is considered to be 'normal'.
● The process is best not rushed – each child needs to develop at their own pace when they are emotionally and physically ready.
● In order to be trained, the child needs to learn what it feels to have a full bladder or bowel, how to link this feeling with 'going' and how to put everything in the right place. There is much more to learn than just sitting on a potty!

How to help
● Keep a diary for a week or two of when the child wet themselves, what was happening at the time and where it happened. This will help you see if there is a pattern.
● Use your diary record to decide when you need to remind the child to 'go'.
● Do not keep asking children if they want the toilet – they will usually say 'no', especially if they are

too busy to stop what they are doing. Instead, ask the child to 'just try' for you at regular intervals.
● Be aware of the signs the child gives you when they need to use the toilet .
● Consider the child's diet. If necessary, ask parents or carers to add more fibre to the diet.
● With daytime 'accidents', stay calm and ask parents/carers to provide a spare pair of pants to bring to the group and a bag for bringing soiled underwear home.
● Make the cloakroom area a pleasant and child-centred place with colourful spaces and the right size and level of fittings.

Finding out more
Positive Parenting: Managing Your 4–8 Year-old by Stockton-on-Tees Educational Psychology Service (QEd Publications) www.qed.uk.com.

WORKING WITH CARERS
● If a child 'wets' during the day, find out from parents or carers whether that child has ever been 'dry' in the past? If so, then you might be seeing wetting because of some recent change in the child's life.

MAKING LINKS
● If there is a soiling problem, talk to the parents and carers about wanting to help them sort this out, and speak with the health visitor if you feel that extra advice is needed.

Trauma

What you need to know

● A trauma can be any distressing event. An important figure in the child's life may have died suddenly or be seriously ill or injured. The child may have been involved in a major incident, such as a bombing, a train crash or other traumatic event.

● Trauma causes an extreme stress reaction that can take its time to settle.

● Each child goes through their own process of readjusting to a traumatic event. Some children may display intense emotions, and others may seem 'frozen' or behave as if nothing was different. All are normal responses. Some will behave as if they were younger, wanting constant cuddles, thumb-sucking and throwing tantrums. This is normal too.

● Sometimes children can become 'stuck' in the process of recovery.

How to help

● Provide a 'secure base' for the child through their period of readjustment. Spend more time with the child and let them be more dependent on you. The need for constant reassurance and physical comfort might be there for several months.

● Provide play experiences to help the child to relieve tension. Younger children find it easiest to share their feelings and ideas through play rather than words. Provide imaginative play, small-world play and picture books, all of which help to make sense of their situation.

● Be there to support the child's play and do not be surprised if play sequences are repeated over and over, perhaps with strong emotion. Keep a diary of their play for a while.

● Maintain familiar routines and sameness. Being with familiar people in a familiar and secure setting is all part of helping the child to realise that their basic security and their sense of who they are can still carry on.

Finding out more

Barnardo's produce the 'Memory Store' and 'Memory Book' for children facing separation, loss and bereavement. Write to: Barnardo's Child Care Publications, Barnardo's Trading Estate, Paycocke Road, Basildon, Essex. SS14 3DR or contact via their website, www.barnardos.org.uk. The Child Bereavement Trust can be contacted at: Aston House, West Wycombe, High Wycombe, Buckinghamshire. HP14 3AG. Send for their information pack. Alternatively, visit their website at www.childbereavement.org.uk, for information, advice and support.

WORKING WITH CARERS

● Do not be afraid to share memories. They are a way of keeping the memory alive and giving a sense of purpose back to the life of the family.

MAKING LINKS

● Be there to listen, to comfort and support family members, perhaps long afterwards.

SPECIAL NEEDS in the early years

Visual impairment

What you need to know

● Some children have difficulty in seeing people and objects clearly unless they are close up and well lit. They are severely near-sighted or 'myopic'. Wearing spectacles helps in this situation.

● Some children can only see clearly at a distance. They may be severely far-sighted or 'presbyopic'. Again, spectacles help.

● Some children have difficulty in co-ordinating the movement of their eyes when tracking, or need to use a patch to make one eye more dominant.

● Some children cannot identify between different colours. Colour-blindness can take different forms.

● Some children have patches of blindness or even tunnel-vision which restricts their field of vision.

● And some children's sight is so restricted that they are effectively 'blind'. About five per cent of children with visual impairment go on to use Braille for reading and writing.

How to help

● Choose brightly coloured toys that attract visual attention.

● Look for playthings that make a sound and are interesting to feel.

● Make sure your spaces are well lit and free from unnecessary clutter and obstacles.

● Have well-defined areas for putting away your toys and materials, so that a child with visual difficulties can always find them.

● Have defined, separate areas for construction equipment, apparatus and physical play so that children with poor sight are safe in quieter areas.

● Use carpeting, curtains and soft furnishings where possible to absorb sound and make sounds easier to hear and to locate.

● Be aware that children whose vision is restricted (and even spectacles restrict your range of vision) may not see you approach. Approach from the front when you can and say the child's name, so that they can identify you from your voice.

● Each adult might use a particular perfume for the child to identify you by as well.

● Sit children with near-sight close to the front in discussions and at story times.

● Look for large-print picture books from your local library.

● Make use of story cassettes and music time.

Finding out more

The Royal National Institute for the Blind can be contacted at: Royal National Institute of the Blind, 105 Judd Street, London, WC1H 9NE Send an sae for their pamphlet and resource list, 'The Early Years' or visit the website, www.rnib.org.

WORKING WITH CARERS

● Talk through your typical session and establish where and when the child might need supporting.

MAKING LINKS

● Most LEAs have support teachers for children with visual impairment – contact the education department for information.

USEFUL CONTACTS

NATIONAL ORGANISATIONS

● Alliance for Inclusive Education, Unit 2, 70 South Lambeth Road, London SW8 1RL. Tel: 020 7735 5277. www.allfie.org.uk.
– Campaigns to end compulsory segregation of children with special education needs within the education system.

● Barnardo's, Tanners Lane, Barkingside, Ilford, Essex IG6 1QG. Tel: 020 8550 8822, www.barnardos.org.uk.
– Provides care and support for children in need and their families, with projects throughout the UK, and distributes useful publications and resources.

● The Child Psychotherapy Trust, Star House, 104–108 Grafton Road, London NW5 4BD.
www.childpsychotherapytrust.org.uk.
– Produces several 'Understanding Childhood' leaflets covering emotional and mental health issues.

● Children in Scotland, Princes House, 5 Shandwick Place, Edinburgh EH2 4RG. Tel: 0131 2288484.
www.childreninscotland.org.uk.
– Holds courses in early years and SEN.

● Children's Society, Edward Rudolf House, Margery Street, London WC1X 0JL.
Tel: 0845 300 11 28.
www.the-childrens-society.org.uk.
– Works with children in need and their families. Runs several family centres and parenting projects.

● The Council for Awards in Children's Care and Education (CACHE) (for Professional Development Award on SEN): 8 Chequer Street, St Alban's, Hertfordshire AL1 3XZ, Tel: 01727 847636.
www.cache.org.uk.

● The Department for Education and Skills (DfES) for parent information and for Government advice and circulars including the SEN Code of Practice and Removing Barriers to Achievement:Tel: 0870 010 40 67 www.dfes.gov.uk.

● The Family Caring Trust, 8 Ashtree Enterprise Park, Newry, Co Down BT34 1BY. www.familycaring.co.uk.
– Publishes the book *From Pram to Primary School* by Micky and Teri Quinn.

● National Association for Special Educational Needs, NASEN House, 4/5 Amber Business Village, Amber Close, Amington, Tamworth, Staffordshire B77 4RP. Tel: 01827 311500.
www.nasen.org.uk.
– Professional association with a database of relevant courses for those wishing to train in SEN. Also supplies the book *The Music Makers Approach: Inclusive Activities for Young Children with Special Educational Needs* by Hannah Mortimer.

● National Children's Bureau, 8 Wakley Street, London EC1V 7QE. Tel: 020 7843 6000. www.ncb.org.uk.
– A multidisciplinary organisation concerned with the promotion and identification of the interests of all children and young people. Involved in research, policy and practice development, and consultancy.

● National Council of Voluntary Child Care Organisations, Unit 4, Pride Court, 80–82 White Lion Street, London N1 9PF. Tel: 020 7833 3319.www.ncvcco.org.
– Umbrella group for voluntary organisations dealing with children.

● National Portage Association for Portage parents and workers, for training in Portage and for information on 'Quality Play' training: Administrator, 127 Monks Dale, Yeovil, Somerset BA21 3JE. www.portage.org.uk.

● National Association of Toy and Leisure Libraries: 68 Churchway, London NW1 1LT. Tel: 020 7255 4600.
www.natll.org.uk.

RESOURCES

● Acorn Educational Ltd at: 32 Queen Eleanor Road, Geddington, Kettering, Northamptonshire NN14 1AY.
Tel: 01536 400212.
www.acorneducational.co.uk.
– Supplies equipment and resources for pre-school early years and special needs.

● Being Yourself (hand puppets and therapeutic games for professionals working to improve mental well-being and emotional literacy in children): send for a catalogue from The Old Bakery, Charlton House, Dour Street, Dover CT16 1ED.
Tel: 01304 226800.
www.smallwood.co.uk.

● CSIE (Centre for Studies on Inclusive Education), New Redland, Frenchay Campus, Coldharbour Lane, Bristol BS16 1QU, http://inclusion.uwe.ac.uk,
– Publishes *Index for Inclusion: Developing Learning and Participation in Schools* by T Booth, M Ainscow, K Black-Hawkins, M Vaughan and L Shaw.

● KCS, FREEPOST, Southampton SO17 1YA, Tel: 023 8058 4314, www.keytools.com.
– Specialist tools for making computer equipment accessible to all children.

● LDA Primary and Special Needs catalogue is available from: Duke Street, Wisbech, Cambridgeshire PE13 2AE. Tel: 01945 463441. www.ldalearning.com.
– Supplies *Circle Time Kit* by Jenny Mosley (puppets, rainstick, magician's cloak and many props for making circle time motivating.)

● Lucky Duck Publishing Ltd.
Tel: 0117 973 2881, www.luckyduck.co.uk.
– Send for a catalogue of videos, SEN books and resources.

● The Magination Press, The Eurospan Group, 3 Henrietta Street, Covent Garden, London WC2E 8LU,
www.maginationpress.com
– Specialises in books which help young children deal with personal or psychological concerns.

● NES Arnold, Novara House, Excelsior Road, Ashby Park, Ashby-de-la-Zouch, LE65 1NG. Tel: 0845 120 45 25.
www.nesarnold.co.uk
– Supplies the *All About Me* materials by Sheila Wolfendale, which can be used to involve children and parents in the assessment process.

● Quality for Effective Development (QEd), The Rom Building, Eastern Avenue, Lichfield, Staffordshire WS13 6RN,
www.qed.uk.com.
– Publishes the books *Playladders* (a checklist of play), *Starting Out* (a talk-through approach to prepare a child with SEN for a new school) and *Taking Part* (talking to a child about statutory assessment) by Hannah Mortimer.

● SBS (Step by Step), Lee Fold, Hyde, Cheshire SK14 4LL. Tel: 0845 3001089, www.sbs-educational.co.uk.
– Supplies toys for all special needs.